A Classical Adventure
The Architectural History of Downing College, Cambridge

This book is dedicated to
the memory of
Sir George Downing, 3rd Baronet,
Founder of the College

and to the many benefactors
who have followed

A Classical Adventure
The Architectural History of Downing College, Cambridge

Tim Rawle

Edited by John Adamson

Photography by Tim Rawle and Louis Sinclair

Aerial perspective drawings by Jeremy Bays and Ed Rawle

Sponsored by the Howard Foundation

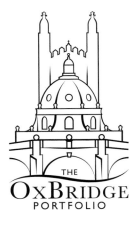

THE
OXBRIDGE
PORTFOLIO

A Classical Adventure: The Architectural History of Downing College, Cambridge

First published 2015; second edition 2018

The Oxbridge Portfolio Ltd
77 Riverside Place
Cambridge CB5 8JF
England

www.oxbridgeportfolio.co.uk

ISBN: 978-0-9572867-5-7

This book was sponsored by the
Howard Foundation, Cambridge

British Library cataloguing in publication data.
A catalogue record for this book is available from the British Library.

Designed and typeset in Granjon by Tim Rawle
Printed by Pureprint, Uckfield, Sussex

Frontispiece: Aerial view of Downing College from the south, May 2014.
Front endpaper: Downing College as it will appear when completed (etching by J. Le Keux after F. Mackenzie). Downing College Archive.
Back endpaper: The intended entrance to the College by R. B. Harraden from the original by William Wilkins. RIBA Library Drawings and Archives Collections.

Contents

Foreword

It was August 1981 and I was a young, newly qualified solicitor on a package holiday with my family, lying on the beach at Albufeira in the Algarve. Suddenly my father appeared above me, beaming, and proffering – unexpectedly – one of the two small bottles of beer he was clutching. He had just made a long-distance call from a *cabine telefônica,* and had confirmation that the Americans had indeed made a commercial success of a slimming product he had spent the last ten years working on. It was the stuff of every inventor's dreams!

You can read elsewhere the story of the wonderfully successful "Cambridge Diet"[1] and how a working-class lad from Norwich came up to Downing in 1948, stayed many years at the University and then established the charitable Howard Foundation,[2] which has invested in pioneering companies, scientific research and, above all else, in Downing. With that little bottle of beer began decades of largesse, of which this book celebrating the architecture of the College is just the latest instance, though we hope not the last.

Tim Rawle's remarkable work charts the turbulent development of an institution that was but a backstop provision in a will. After ferocious opposition, Downing was left nearly destitute for well over a century, a tragedy when one contemplates what could have been achieved had the original eighteenth-century Downing family fortune, worth some £100 million in today's money, not been squandered. Over the last thirty or so years, benefactors such as ourselves, and others you will read about, have in effect re-founded and stabilised the College by providing facilities which are not only essential for College life but, wherever possible, are income-producing. I jokingly ask College staff about their 'Hilton Hotel' and Conference Centre with Costa Coffee outlet, but in fact Downing has merely shown a way for academic institutions in the contemporary world to utilise their improved facilities commercially. In Downing's case the income generated by the Howard buildings helps make up for the endowment never received; and of course we are only part of a modern history of donations from generous alumni and associates who have funded renovation, new facilities, scholarships, indeed anything needed, and that is why this book is dedicated to these College benefactors.

With wealth come great choices. Many successful businessmen sail away to tax exile, donating the occasional gift to charity. In emulating Wellcome[3] we sought to act as a modern role model – indeed, in timely fashion given the Thatcherite revolution and Dotcom-type bonanzas that followed. However, we have been assisted by the College itself, which has nearly always honoured its classical tradition, and fought hard to ensure that any new facilities provided are aesthetically appropriate, practical for College life, easily maintained, and part of its ethos of being accessible to all.

I went back to Albufeira for the first time a couple of years ago and was shocked to find a ghastly concrete jungle of overdevelopment and bad planning: they had certainly blown the opportunity that the investment of the last thirty years could have achieved. In contrast, Downing is not just the good-looking set of buildings you will now see and read about, but also a very distinctive and vibrant collegiate community of excellence, which those who fought to found it could scarcely have imagined, and of which all with links are proud to be a part.

Jon Howard
Secretary of the Howard Foundation
May 2018

1 See *The Cambridge Diet* by Alan Howard (Jonathan Cape, 1985, ISBN 0 224 02314 4) and <http://www.cambridgeweightplan.com>.
2 See <http://www.howard-foundation.com>.
3 See *Henry Wellcome* by Robert Rhodes James (Hodder & Stoughton, 1994, ISBN 0 340 60617 7) and <http://www.wellcome.ac.uk>.

2. *(opposite page) Detail from main doorway of the Howard Building, the first Howard Foundation building at Downing College.*

3. The West Range   (overleaf: 4. The East Range)

Introduction and acknowledgements

In November 2013, Alan Howard rang me out of the blue from Cannes to see if I would be attending the memorial service in College on the 23rd for a much-loved Downing Fellow, Richard Stibbs. That date to celebrate Richard's life had been firmly in my diary for some time, and was now to be combined with a brief, but fascinating discussion that Richard, of all people, would have found very exciting: an idea to produce a book on the architectural story of Downing. By Christmas, I had agreed with Alan and his son, Jon, to write and illustrate a book that they wanted to be "enjoyable to all": something that was easily readable; half pictures half text, or better still with more pictures than text; colourful, bright and informative. As an undergraduate who had read architecture at Downing many years ago, and now an architectural photographer and writer, I was delighted to be given this wonderful opportunity. I had always admired the buildings of William Wilkins, and especially the ambience of this beautiful place that he had created and where I spent three years of my life. It has been a great privilege to undertake this commission that is yet another extraordinary gift of the Howard Foundation to the College, and now in a new second edition.

I thought I knew much about Downing until I started to do serious research – I could then have created a book twice the size – happily, I was steered into achieving something that I hope is indeed an enjoyable end result for all. Whilst I have attempted to tread a neutral path, any views expressed are my own as someone who is simply taking stock at this point in the College's history, and I hope that in the few instances where there is anything bordering on the controversial, it may lead to healthy debate and constructive progress in the future.

I am indebted to many people over the last few years for all their help and guidance. I would like to express my sincere thanks and gratitude to Alan and Jon Howard for their patience and for allowing me such a free hand throughout the project. There are four key people without whose help this book would have been so much harder to complete: my incredibly thorough, supportive editor and long-time stalwart friend, colleague and publishing consultant, John Adamson; my brilliant young co-photographer, Louis Sinclair; James Gascoigne, who together with his team at Pureprint have done the most amazing job both times; and my partner, Anita Dullaert, whose practical help as lay reader and

commentator, along with her general moral support, were ever encouraging. The wonderful aerial perspectives of the college on pages 12–13 and 60–1 were drawn by Jeremy Bays. The stunning new aerial view of a potential Downing of the future (pp. 184–5) was drawn by my son, Edward, with the help of Paul Jordan and Fahran Younas of Blackpoint Design.

I would like to thank the Master and Fellows of Downing for allowing unrestricted access to buildings and archives, and I owe a special debt of gratitude to: Geoffrey Grimmett (Master), Paul Millett (Vice-Master), David Pratt, Susan Lintott (Bursar) and Jenny Ulph for reading my manuscript. As Archivist, Jenny has provided the most invaluable help throughout the project. Any lapses of fact remaining are wholly my responsibility. I am also very grateful to: the Bursar's assistant, Lindsey Chalmers; the former Junior Bursar, Dick Taplin, an endless source of knowledge on the everyday life of Downing buildings; Karen Lubarr and her colleagues in the Library; Gabrielle Bennett, former Development Director, and her colleagues in the Development Office; Jacqui Cressey, former Conferences Manager, and her colleagues in the Conference Office; Barrie Hunt and Norman Berger of the Downing Association; Prerona Prasad, Exhibitions Officer and Gallery Supervisor in the Heong Gallery; the Head Porter, Tina D'Angelico, and her colleagues in the Porters' Lodge; the grounds staff; the catering and kitchen staff for emptying the Hall of all furniture between Christmas and New Year 2014 for photography; Martin Bandkowski and his colleagues in the Howard Theatre; and Richard Monument and his colleagues of the Maintenance and Buildings Department.

Outside the College there are a number of people I especially wish to thank: Sir James Dyson for the helicopter ride over Downing for aerial photographs in May 2014; my digital expert colleague, Craig Dallas, for his recent help with picture improvements in this second edition; the Revd Felicity Couch for access to All Saints Church, Croydon, Cambridgeshire; Sebastian Kindersley for access to St Denis Church, East Hatley, Cambridgeshire; and Gale Glynn for her comments on the coat of arms at St Denis Church.

Tim Rawle, May 2018

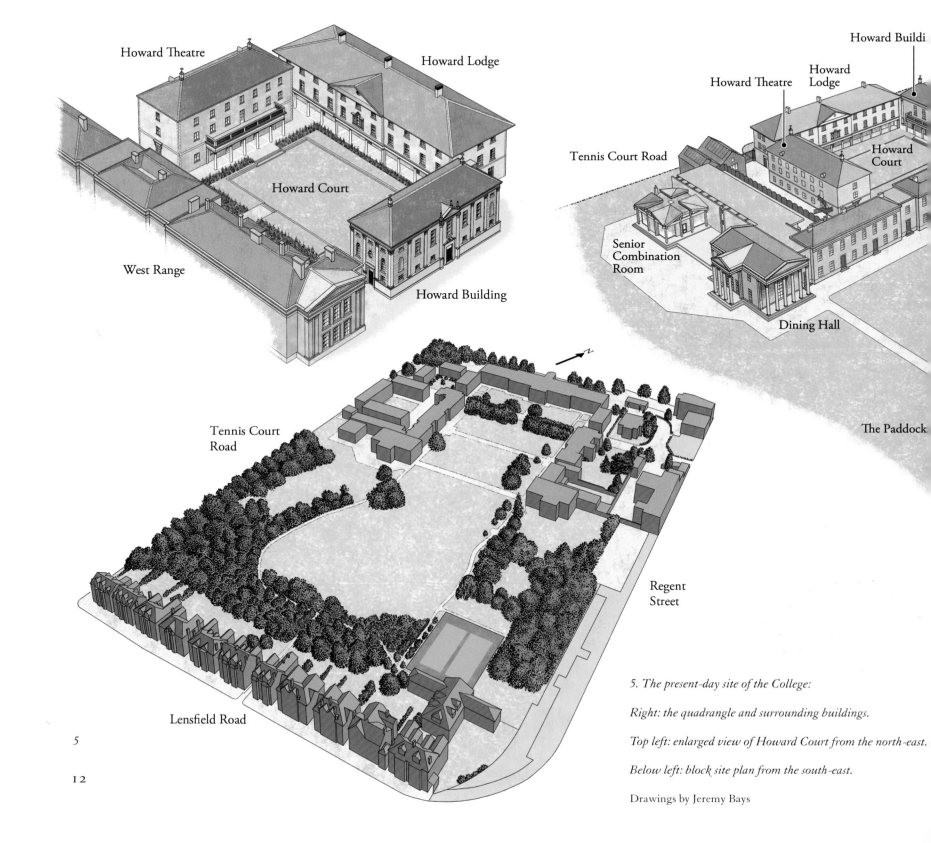

Howard Theatre

Howard Lodge

Howard Court

West Range

Howard Building

Howard Buildi

Howard Theatre

Howard Lodge

Howard Buildi

Tennis Court Road

Howard Court

Senior
Combination
Room

Dining Hall

The Paddock

Tennis Court
Road

Regent
Street

Lensfield Road

5

12

5. The present-day site of the College:

Right: the quadrangle and surrounding buildings.

Top left: enlarged view of Howard Court from the north-east.

Below left: block site plan from the south-east.

Drawings by Jeremy Bays

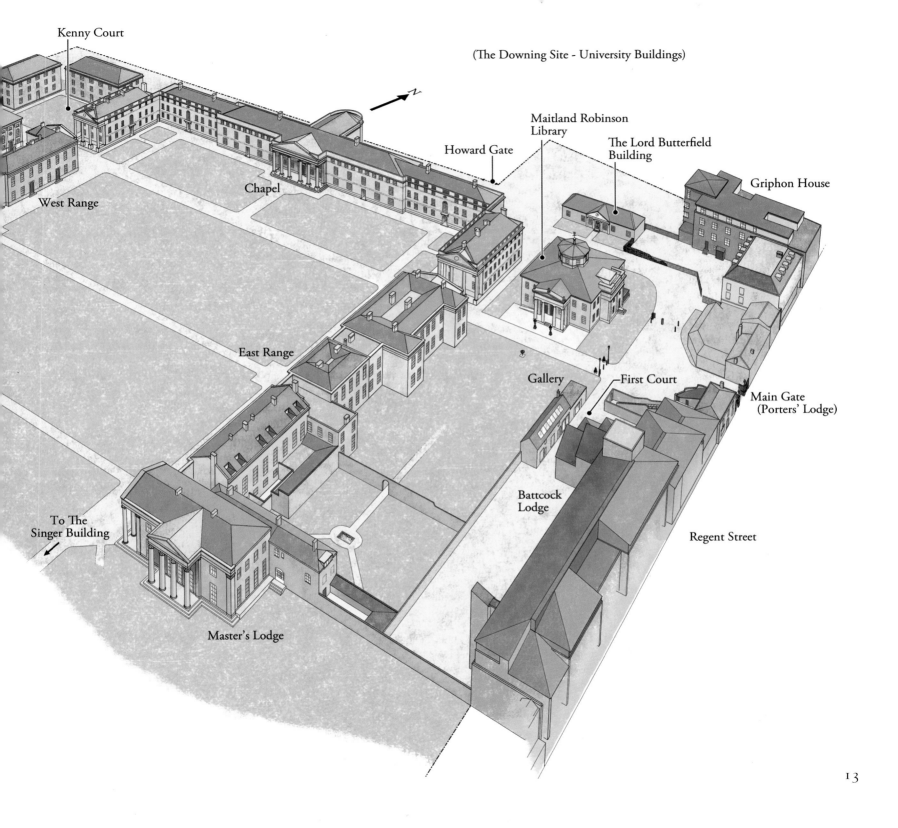

Kenny Court

(The Downing Site - University Buildings)

Maitland Robinson
Library

Howard Gate

The Lord Butterfield
Building

Griphon House

Chapel

West Range

East Range

Gallery

First Court

Main Gate
(Porters' Lodge)

Battcock
Lodge

To The
Singer Building

Regent Street

Master's Lodge

13

I The Cambridge colleges before 1800 and Downing

Viewing Cambridge from a thousand feet over the city centre (figs. 6 and 7) gives one a feeling of being transported back in time by several hundred years. The interconnecting clusters of buildings have changed little in their layout since medieval times, and extensive Victorian, even modern, additions to those precincts have followed the original layout of the enclosed, or semi-enclosed, courtyard. It is possible to see how whole college sites have gradually evolved, in some cases over six to seven hundred years, from an original, single building into the extensive compositions of today; a unique development within the British universities that exists only in the two ancient foundations of Oxford and Cambridge.

In looking more closely at the pictures, even from such a height it is easy to see that the Gothic style of architecture dominates. This style came to England from the Continent about eight hundred years ago, and in the hands of English masons reached its zenith in the third and final stage of its development: Perpendicular Gothic, often considered to be the true historical style of England and thus appropriate

6. Cambridge city centre from the south-east.

7. Cambridge city centre from the west. The site of Downing College is just visible in the top right-hand corner of the picture.

7

8

for the design of "Oxbridge" colleges. One of the finest examples of this style can be seen in the centre of the pictures, King's College Chapel of 1446–1515, which dominates the Cambridge skyline (fig. 8). Yet, if one scans the pictures in more detail, it is also possible to see the influence of the Mediterranean style of classical architecture that was gradually introduced to England just after the reign of Henry VIII and began to compete seriously with Gothic from the seventeenth century; it is apparent in such buildings as the Library at Trinity College or Gibbs' Building at King's. For well over two hundred years the Gothic host was being augmented piecemeal by the classical intruder, until the radical concept of Downing College, as a complete, self-contained classical composition, employing a new and innovatory plan, entered the scene in the early nineteenth century.

The early colleges – plan and style

In thirteenth-century Cambridge there were no university departments or colleges as we know them today. Teachers rented rooms in private houses in which to teach, and students rented lodgings and lived among the townspeople, but soon formed their own hostels, eventually living in colleges with their teachers. It was not until the mid-fourteenth century that the University started to construct buildings used specifically for teaching, in what today is the small courtyard known as the "Old Schools" in the centre of the town (figs. 9 and 10). This relatively tiny complex was to remain the only visual reference to the University in Cambridge for the next two hundred and fifty years, and was to be considerably dwarfed by the many associated colleges that were soon to surround it. Cambridge, like Oxford, has always been a city dominated by colleges, not by the University itself, which cannot be identified as a single physical entity in the same way that a college can, though the two are inextricably linked. To the visitor unacquainted with either place, the presence of the "University" is not immediately obvious, with the ceremonial, administrative and departmental buildings scattered throughout each city, both of which are effectively extensive university campuses.

At first, there was no organised plan for the building of a college in either Oxford or Cambridge. The essential components for a college community were studies and bedrooms for the fellows, and later also for the students; a house for the head of the college, normally called a master's lodge; a library which, initially, was no more than a room with books in it; kitchens and a refectory, or dining-hall; and a chapel, though nearby parish churches often sufficed until dedicated chapels followed later.

9

10

8. *Cambridge centre looking south, with King's College Chapel dominating the skyline.*

9. *The medieval Old Schools precinct from the east, behind the eighteenth-century buildings in front, with the former King's College Old Court gatehouse visible. King's Chapel is to the south, dwarfing these original University buildings.*

10. *The oldest University building in Cambridge, the Divinity School (c. 1350–1400), part of the Old Schools.*

Although the layout grew organically, a number of models have been suggested as playing an important role in the early development of the college plan. The most obvious inspiration was that of the monastic courtyard, and that similarity strongly pervades the atmosphere of many of the ancient colleges of both universities; such as, in Cambridge, Old Court at Corpus Christi College (fig. 11), built between 1352 and *circa* 1377, and Front Court at Queens' of 1448–9 (fig. 12).

Among other sources of inspiration for the design and layout of the ancient colleges were the medieval manor house and, going back even further, the English castle. The nineteenth-century historians Robert Willis and John Willis Clark postulated a strong connection between the great manor houses of the fifteenth century, and particularly that of a specific country house, Haddon Hall in Derbyshire, which they related to the two older courts of Queens' College.[1] Though more a small castle in feel, Haddon Hall bears a remarkable likeness to an ancient Oxbridge college, and the putative influence of that building type on the early collegiate designers is convincing. Nevertheless, the feature common to the majority of college layouts is that of buildings enclosing a rectangular space to create a quadrangle or courtyard, by convention called a "quad" at Oxford, and a "court" at Cambridge. The organic growth of the colleges over so many centuries has given rise to extensive groups of buildings and an extraordinary way of academic life that would be impossible to replicate in a new university. At the same time, this gradual evolution has had a deep and lasting influence on the architecture characteristic of these two cities and, as we have already seen, the style of that architecture was overwhelmingly Gothic. The rise of Gothic architecture thus coincided with the emergence of the two ancient universities and shaped their older colleges.

After the first group of Cambridge colleges – from Peterhouse in 1284 to Corpus Christi in 1352 – there were no further colleges for almost a hundred years, but we then see the birth of the biggest foundations from the 1440s to the mid-sixteenth century. The next major development was the creation of what has arguably become the most famous of all Oxbridge colleges: King's College, Cambridge, founded by Henry VI in 1441. At the outset, Henry's idea for a small college of a rector and twelve scholars was modest,[2] and building proceeded on such a scale with what is now known as King's Old Court, part of the Old Schools precinct to the north of the famous chapel. A few years later Henry revised his ideas in favour of a much larger foundation, one that in the sheer number of its projected members was to be on a scale hitherto unseen in either university. He expanded his existing

11

12

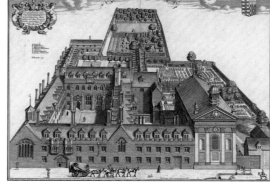

13

11. *Old Court, Corpus Christi College.*
12. *The front of Queens' College Old Court.*
13 and 14. *Loggan's engravings of Pembroke and St John's Colleges, c. 1675.*
15. *The Gate of Honour, Gonville and Caius College.*

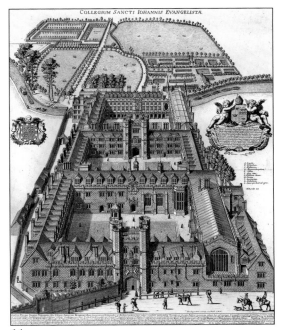

14

15

site to the south over a tract of the densely populated town centre, and by compulsory purchase demolished the whole network of housing and lanes that stretched from the High Street (now King's Parade) down to the river, as well as all the wharves. This royal intervention was to change for ever the character of the small market town, and marked the start of its transformation into a huge university campus and the inevitable co-habitation of "Town and Gown".

The great artist and engraver, David Loggan (1634–1692), left an invaluable record of both Oxford and Cambridge colleges as aerial perspectives, from which we can see the compact and enclosed layouts of the medieval foundations, such as Cambridge's Pembroke and St John's as they were in the late seventeenth century (figs. 13 and 14).[3]

The next important development in both planning and architecture, followed when Dr John Caius re-founded his alma mater of Gonville Hall, as Gonville and Caius College in 1557, and built Caius Court in 1565–7. This was a second court, preconceived, planned and built with a totally new conception in mind and buildings that reflected his continental experiences, after several years travelling widely and studying medicine in Italy. As a physician, Caius deliberately planned his court as a three-sided composition, leaving the south side open with only a wall and gateway; the idea being that air could enter and flow freely around the space in order to aid hygiene, bearing in mind how insalubrious urban living would have been at this time with frequent outbreaks of plague. This three-sided court layout became known as the "sanitary plan" and was used many times thereafter in both universities, though later more on grounds of aesthetics than health. Caius also built three classically inspired gates to his own designs that charmingly symbolise the three-year passage of the student through the College: the Gates of Humility, Virtue and Honour (fig. 15). Here were the earliest buildings in Cambridge to herald the arrival of the new, Mediterranean style, albeit on a small scale.

The creation of the two Elizabethan colleges in the late sixteenth century, Emmanuel (1584) and Sidney Sussex (1596), marked the end of a three-hundred-year continuum of major college foundations, beginning with Peterhouse in 1284. No further colleges were established for more than two centuries until Downing in 1800, but in the interim some of Cambridge's finest and most beautiful buildings were added to existing foundations.

Classical architecture invades Cambridge

The "neo-classical" style of architecture was born of the Renaissance, that extraordinary cultural rebirth in the history of Europe of the fourteenth to seventeenth century, inspired by the science, art, literature and architecture of the ancient world. Starting in Italy and then spreading through Europe, it effectively formed a cultural bridge between the medieval and modern ages. This revival of interest in antiquity resulted in a new flowering of the arts and the birth of modern science. In architecture, the reference was to ancient Greece and Rome, and to the classical style of those great civilisations, with buildings governed by strict rules of proportion and harmony accompanied by an essential uniform, or "dress" – without which they could not be wholly classical – derived from the five "orders" of Tuscan, Doric, Ionic, Corinthian and Composite. This complex language and vocabulary – what Sir John Summerson dubbed the "Latin of Architecture"[4] – gave widespread rise to buildings of a very different appearance to those of the Gothic style. Classical architecture in Italy at this time was based in part on principles taken from surviving buildings from antiquity and on the ten-volume treatise by Vitruvius (Marcus Vitruvius Pollio), a Roman architect of the first century BC. Renaissance architects and theorists then developed the "new" classical style that spread to France, Germany and the Netherlands and crossed the sea to England, where it greatly influenced architects such as Inigo Jones (1573–1652) and Christopher Wren (1632–1723). Out of this interest in the ancient world grew the "Grand Tour": for any cultured and wealthy young man to experience at first hand the art and architecture of the Mediterranean countries became a fashionable accomplishment, and for any aspiring architect of the period a necessity.

In Cambridge it took some time before major buildings began to appear that were predominantly in the new fashion; there was a period when an entertaining blend of Gothic and classical motifs and details were often to be found in the same façades as designers strove to leave their old traditions behind and embrace the new style. This began in the second quarter of the seventeenth century when a group of hybrid buildings were built, signalling the beginning of the invasion in earnest. This transitional phase from Gothic to classical can be seen in such buildings as Peterhouse Chapel (1628–32, fig. 16), the rebuilt court of Clare College (1638–1715, fig. 17), and the first almost wholly classical building in Cambridge, Fellows' Building at Christ's College (1640–3, fig. 18). Here, for the first time, was a large, detached building overwhelmingly classical in its symmetrical composition and

16

17

18

16. *Peterhouse Chapel.*
17. *Clare College from the south, with the Chapel of King's College towering above.*
18. *Fellows' Building, Christ's College.*

19

20

21

19. *Pepys Building, Magdalene College.*
20. *Clare College Bridge.*
21. *The 'Wren' Bridge, St John's College.*

detail, with hardly any allusion to the Gothic past. Located to the east of the original Old Court of the College in a garden setting, this building was also a distinct deviation from the traditional expansion of the courtyard system, for it did not lend itself to the obvious extension of a second court, but rather made an individual statement as a separate, free-standing building set within the surrounding landscape. A brief propensity to build detached classical ranges occurs at this time, such as Pepys Building at Magdalene College (fig. 19), completed around 1688.[5]

At about the same time as the landmark Fellows' Building at Christ's College, a local master mason, Thomas Grumbold (d. 1657), built another fine classical structure in Cambridge, Clare College Bridge of 1639–40 (fig. 20), the oldest bridge over the river. In that same year, Robert Grumbold (1639–1720) was born, a kinsman of the older man[6] and likewise a mason, who was later to become a local protégé of Wren when employed on Trinity College Library. In 1709–12 he also built a beautiful classical bridge, this time at St John's and known as the Old Bridge or the "Wren" Bridge (fig. 21), as it was heavily influenced by both Wren and Nicholas Hawksmoor.[7]

It was at this time that England's greatest classical architect, Christopher Wren (1632–1723), appeared on the scene in Cambridge. He was only 31 when his uncle, Dr Matthew Wren, a Fellow of Pembroke, commissioned him to design a new chapel for the college. Built in 1663–5 with an elegant façade to Trumpington Street, this was his first-ever completed building (fig. 22). Wren returned twice to Cambridge over the next twenty-five years to build Emmanuel College Chapel in 1666–73 (fig. 23), followed by Trinity College Library in 1679–90, his Cambridge masterpiece (fig. 24). His buildings in Cambridge from the latter half of the seventeenth century were thereafter to have a profound influence on local architects and masons. One such architect was James Essex who, in 1769–75, completely rebuilt the west range of Emmanuel College to harmonise with Wren's chapel, creating the most dominantly classical collegiate street façade in Cambridge (fig. 25).

The quiet eighteenth century in Cambridge

After this flurry of activity in Cambridge through the middle and later years of the seventeenth century, things quietened down in the eighteenth century and little of importance happened architecturally, other than two exceptional buildings by another prominent architect of the period, James Gibbs (1682–1754). He designed the first university building – as opposed to collegiate – to be built in Cambridge for over 250 years, the Senate House of 1722–30 (fig. 26). This striking building brought a new elegance to the public face of both the University and the town. It was a further, definitive statement post-Wren that classical architecture proper had now firmly arrived in this out-of-the-way East Anglian market-town-with-a-university. After the Senate House, Gibbs built Fellows' Building at King's College in 1724–9, soon to become known as Gibbs' Building (fig. 27), reflecting this architect's considerable stature. The rest of King's Front Court was to be completed a hundred years later, with an extensive south range and the highly acclaimed Gothic Revival screen to King's Parade (fig. 28), all designed by the next architect in our story, William Wilkins.

Within the overall plan of King's, an innovatory aspect of Gibbs' Building was the placing of it as an independent range at right angles to, and separated from, the magnificent chapel. The building today is flanked to the east by the large lawn of Front Court and the Gothic screen to the street and, more importantly, to the west by the open space of the formal lawn that stretches down to the river with the idyllic pastoral scene of Scholars' Piece beyond, the iconic view of Cambridge that is known worldwide (see fig. 29). This is undoubtedly one of the most successful examples of spacious collegiate planning in either university. The dramatic effect of a large, low, single classical building set next to the tall epitome of Perpendicular Gothic, within an open landscape and space flowing freely around the buildings, must have been inspirational for the next generation of architects who were soon to follow, seeking to break away from the age-old Cambridge tradition of small, enclosed courtyards.

The battle of the styles and the birth of a new college

This brings us to the middle years of the Georgian era (1714–1830) and to a fascinating period in English architectural history where we encounter what came to be known as the "battle of the styles". As we have seen, Gothic architecture dominated Cambridge for many centuries, until the Italian Renaissance swept Europe and neo-classical architecture made its gradual appearance in the town from the mid-1600s, becoming firmly established by the end of that century. A new competition between the two styles emerged in the late eighteenth century, when the supremacy of Classicism, which had become the embodiment of good taste in society, was challenged by a major Gothic Revival. At roughly the same time, there

22

23

22-4: The Cambridge buildings of Christopher Wren:
Pembroke College Chapel (22);
Emmanuel College Chapel (23);
Trinity College Library (24).

25. The street front of Emmanuel College by
James Essex.

24

was renewed interest in ancient Greece, again referring archaeologists, artists and architects back to the roots of classical antiquity.

The Greek Revival marked the last stage in the development of neo-classical architecture in England, and the "battle" that ensued between the styles ran well into the next century, not only between the mainstream Gothic and Classical camps, but within the classical factions themselves: between the new Graecophils focusing on archaeological correctness from antiquity, against the now stale and moderate Palladians (after Andrea Palladio 1508–1580). All this coincided with the sequence of events leading up to the eventual founding of Downing College in 1800, and to a competition to design its buildings during this lively period of stylistic conflict.

We have touched on two architects, James Essex and William Wilkins, both of whom were to be involved in the long process to design this new college, the first to be founded in Cambridge for more than two hundred years. Though not of the same generation – Essex died in 1784, Wilkins was born in 1778 – they came from similar backgrounds and were both trained in the Gothic and Classical: Essex, the son of a local carpenter and joiner, who had attended the grammar school attached to King's College and then served as an apprentice under Sir James Burrough, an academic and amateur architect in the Palladian manner; Wilkins, the son of a

25

Norwich builder and self-taught architect, who had ascended to a place at the University to study mathematics at Gonville and Caius College (1796–1800) and then proceeded into the architectural profession. A recognised authority on Gothic as well as a competent classicist, the older Essex was approaching the end of his career; Wilkins was the bright young academic who had been awarded a travel scholarship after graduation and had embarked on a grand tour to Greece, Asia Minor and Italy. It was to be the younger man who eventually rose successfully to the challenge.

The architectural scene in central Cambridge in the latter half of the eighteenth and early nineteenth century must have been an inspiring place for any young architect, surrounded by both old Gothic and "modern" Classical. It was a time when architects needed to be versatile in their training, able to design in both the style of old England as well as the neo-classical inspired by antiquity via contemporary Italy, and now with a new focus on all things Greek. It is intriguing to imagine the young Wilkins in a Georgian Cambridge in surroundings where the huge Gothic chapel of King's held sway, but where the more recent neo-classical achievements of Wren and Gibbs asserted their presence, and to ponder the influence these buildings must have had on him. How easy it would have been for him to wander out of his own College precinct under the shadow of King's, down the lanes towards the river, through the rebuilt court of neighbouring Clare and across Thomas Grumbold's beautiful classical bridge into the fields of west Cambridge. At that point we can readily picture him looking back across the water-meadows of the Backs towards the dramatic composition of Gibbs's Building adjacent to King's Chapel (fig. 29), taking in the "shock of the new" and wondering what he might possibly do with it. Five architects were to put forward schemes for Downing College. We will see how Wilkins' proposal finally won the day and established the Greek Revival as the dominant style of the period.

Notes
1 Willis and Clark, vol. III, p. 270.
2 Pevsner, p. 92.
3 David Loggan, *Oxonia Illustrata*, 1675 and *Cantabrigia Illustrata*, c. 1690.
4 Summerson, p. 7.
5 Named after the celebrated diarist Samuel Pepys (1633–1703), who bequeathed his library of books to the College in 1703, including his diaries.
6 Colvin, p. 367.
7 Bradley and Pevsner, p. 200.

26

27

28

26. *The Senate House by James Gibbs.*
27. *Gibbs' Building at King's College, by James Gibbs.*
28. *The Gothic screen at King's by William Wilkins.*

29. King's College Chapel and Gibbs' Building from the Backs.

2 Born of a romantic age: Downing, last of the old colleges, first of the new

The origin of Downing College can be traced back to an arranged marriage between two aristocratic children in the year 1700, the sad and barren outcome of which would ultimately result in the foundation of the College a hundred years later. Little is known of this wedding, which took place in hushed circles in Shropshire, other than that on a winter's day in February of that year a pretty young girl of thirteen named Mary Forester became the bride of her cousin, George Downing, who was fifteen.[1] This boy, the eventual founder of the College, was the grandson of George Downing, 1st Baronet, who had brought both fame and fortune to the family name and had been knighted by Charles II in 1660; but the newly titled line was only to survive 104 years, until the death of the fourth and last baronet in 1764. Though the first Sir George is by far the most colourful and interesting character in our story, without whose self-made fortune there would have been no college to found, there were many other characters whose lives had an impact on how Downing College is here today.

A brief history of the Downing family: four baronets and their ladies

The Downings hailed from Suffolk in the east of England, and in the reign of Henry VIII we find a George Downing (1525–1564) living on the Suffolk/Norfolk border in Beccles on Waveney, seventeen miles south-east of Norwich on the southern edge of the Norfolk Broads.[2] A profound belief in education was already apparent, a creed that would run through the Downing family for generations. George's two sons, George and John, were well provided for and educated at the local grammar school before attending the University of Cambridge some sixty miles away. Son George (1556–1611) entered Queens' College in 1569, graduated in 1573, and proceeded to MA at Corpus Christi College four years later. From 1589 to 1610 he was headmaster of the Grammar School in Ipswich. He too was clearly well-to-do and while his three daughters all married into good families, his four sons went into the professions: Emanuel became a lawyer; Nathaniel a London businessman; Joseph a churchman as Rector of St Stephens, Ipswich; and Joshua a Commissioner of the Navy and a Justice of the Peace. This eldest son was not christened George after the father in the family tradition, but was named Emanuel in honour of his father's University and its newest college of that name founded in Cambridge in 1584, the year before his birth.

30. "Collegium Dunense": an etching of the proposed Master's Lodge of Downing, reflecting the style and romance of the period. Downing College Archive.

Emanuel Downing (1585–c.1660) was educated at Ipswich Grammar School, and on 16 December 1602 was admitted scholar to Trinity Hall, Cambridge, a college renowned for the teaching of law.[3] He then became a barrister in the Inner Temple, London, and in 1614 married Anne Ware, daughter of Sir James Ware, who was posted to Dublin in 1616 as Ireland Secretary to James I. Emanuel and Anne soon followed Sir James to Ireland and Emanuel practised law there for several years. Anne bore them three children, but died in 1620. In 1622 Emanuel then married Lucy Winthrop, daughter of Adam and Anne Winthrop, in Groton, Suffolk, and the newlyweds continued to live in Dublin where the first son of that marriage, George, was born circa 1623. Returning to London in 1625, they lived in Fleet Street and then Lincoln's Field, and had six more children. Emanuel developed an important and life-long friendship with his brother-in-law, John Winthrop, a graduate of Trinity College, Cambridge (1602–5), both of them practising as attorneys in the Court of Wards and Liveries. In 1629 John Winthrop emigrated to New England, where he became the first Governor of the Massachusetts Bay Colony, of which Emanuel Downing was a strong supporter and for which he served as legal adviser.[4] The Downing family followed, settling in Salem, Massachusetts, in 1638, when George was fourteen or fifteen. George was enrolled at a new school, and in 1644 achieved his BA amongst the first graduates of Harvard University, reputedly staying there for a while as one of the college's first tutors.[5] It was from this point that his extraordinary, multi-professional career began: college tutor; preacher and military chaplain; spymaster, soldier and diplomat under Oliver Cromwell; MP for several Scottish and English seats; and finally diplomat and Puritan statesman under Charles II. Moreover, throughout his whole adult life he held many powerful and lucrative public office positions that for decades gave him an exceptionally good income and rich pickings. Such a confident, shrewd and opportunistic operator was Downing, that he managed to steer a brilliantly successful career through the turbulent years of the English Civil War and the Interregnum – while operating as a staunch supporter of the Parliamentarian cause and surviving the end of the Cromwells and the Rump Parliament – and then astonishingly regained favour with Charles II at the Restoration.

When George Downing left Massachusetts in 1645, aged about twenty-two, he sailed back to England via the West Indies as chaplain on a slave-ship, and was noted for his preaching in Barbados and elsewhere en route.[6] On his return in 1646 he obtained a further post as chaplain, this time in one of Cromwell's regiments in Scotland under Colonel John Okey, who had been a family acquaintance of the Downings before they left for New England and had sponsored young George's education in Massachusetts.

Okey was to be one of the fifty-nine regicides who signed Charles I's death warrant. Under Okey, Downing got a taste for army life and quickly rose through the Roundhead ranks to be made Scoutmaster General in 1649, effectively Head of Intelligence with the rank of a major general. So committed to the Parliamentarian cause was Downing that he fought in two of the main battles of the Civil War: at Dunbar in 1650, where he was wounded; and at Worcester in 1651, where Cromwell's "Model Army" defeated the Royalist forces of Charles II in what was to be the final battle of the conflict. In 1654 he achieved a good marriage, as befitted his social ambitions, to Frances Howard, said to be a great beauty, daughter of Sir William Howard and sister of the first Earl of Carlisle. He then turned his hand to politics and in that year became MP for Edinburgh, followed by Carlisle in 1656–60 and Morpeth in 1660–84. His diplomatic career also started in 1655 when Cromwell appointed him Envoy Extraordinary to France, though he was still operating as Scoutmaster General and based in Westminster.

In 1658 the most important period of Downing's political career as an international diplomat began when he was appointed Cromwell's Resident at The Hague, the first of three terms over the following twelve years. Downing was thrown into the complexities of European political affairs, his main task being to deal with the difficult Anglo-Dutch naval situation, the Dutch being the main commercial rivals of England at this time. He engaged in a long battle over trade routes, lending his steadfast support to the Navigation Acts that strengthened England's command of the seas. In his lengthy dealings with the Dutch it is quite possible he may have been involved in brokering the acquisition from them of New York, as there are Downing Streets named after him in both Manhattan and Brooklyn. All along he was still operating a thorough intelligence network at home and on the continent, engaging in the activities of the exiled Stuarts (the Royal family), in the United Provinces (Holland) and France.

Downing, more aware than many of the oncoming Restoration, is said to have done Charles Stuart a service that greatly helped him regain the favour of the future king. The story goes that one night, while accommodated by the Dutch in Brussels, Charles went in disguise on a clandestine visit to The Hague to see his sister, the Princess of Orange; though other versions say it was to visit his mother, Henrietta Maria of France, widow of Charles I. Charles Stuart and his only companion, Lord Falkland, had put up at an inn for the night when they were approached by the landlord and told that a beggar was asking permission to see them on a matter of great urgency.

On being admitted, the man tore off his false beard and fell on his knees, introducing himself as Mr Downing, the Resident of Oliver Cromwell at The Hague. Downing revealed that he had received intelligence of this secret visit by His Majesty, and warned that if Charles ventured any further he would be assassinated. He pleaded secrecy for fear of his own life and swiftly departed. Whether the intelligence was true or not, Downing was so convincing that Charles and Lord Falkland were wholly taken in and, proceeding no further, returned to Brussels clearly indebted to Downing for this intervention.[7]

Some years later, Downing enlisted the help of his brother-in-law, Thomas Howard, Earl of Carlisle, to make a presentation to the king in April 1660 on Downing's behalf, offering his services. The wording employed clearly hints at the behaviour of a potential double-agent. Carlisle swore to the king that Downing "never had any malice to your Majesty's person or family".[8] Furthermore, around this same time Carlisle stated that Downing was reported to have said in correspondence with Cromwell's Secretary of State, about the king's intentions, that he "has given an answer with all imaginable advantage to the King", so supporting the notion that Downing was indeed playing a double game, working from both sides for his own gain.[9]

Downing was knighted by Charles II in 1660 and made a baronet in 1663 (fig. 31), when he was endowed with a large estate, including land in Whitehall, London, upon which he built Downing Street between 1682 and 1684. This was all much to the disgust of contemporary diarists such as John Evelyn, who recorded that Downing "had ben a great . . . [traitor] against his Ma[ty] [Majesty] but now insinuated into his favour, and from a pedagogue and fanatic preacher not worth a groate, had become excessive rich".[10] Number 10 has been the official residence of prime ministers since Sir Robert Walpole, regarded as Britain's first prime minister (1721–42). Winston Churchill quipped that the houses in Downing Street were "shaky and lightly built by the profiteering contractor whose name they bear"[11] and John Major on the BBC in 2014 referred to Sir George Downing as an original "rogue landlord".[12] All this notwithstanding, a portrait of him still hangs just inside the famous front door.

After the Restoration Downing continued in his role at The Hague, but things did not always go as planned. Though now a knight and a baronet, and considering himself a man of stature, Sir George was unhappy with the way he was being treated by the States General when back at The Hague. Pepys recorded that he openly complained that "he was not received with the respect and observance now, that he

31

31. Sir George Downing, first Baronet. Harvard Art Museums/Fogg Museum.

was when he came from the traitor and rebell Cromwell".[13] Though an able and successful diplomat, Downing had many enemies and it is believed that several assassination attempts were made on him. In often heated negotiations with the Dutch authorities, undoubtedly with underhand tactics of his own contrivance and his associated agents over many years taking place in the background, he became extremely unpopular with the States General and the people themselves. This all came to a head in his last term at The Hague in the winter of 1671–2 when he was expelled and had to make a quick exit in fear for his life from the mob, returning home to England without the consent of the king, who had sensed that Downing was not working in his best interests. Charles was not amused, and immediately on arrival Downing was sent to the Tower. By many at home he was deemed a traitor to the Parliamentarian cause, particularly for his betrayal of former colleagues and his hunting down of certain regicides who had fled to the continent in 1660. One of three, Okey, his erstwhile family friend, sponsor and commander, was hanged, drawn and quartered: the punishment for high treason. Samuel Pepys, the diarist, who knew Downing well and had served under him as one of his clerks since 1656, likened him to a "perfidious rogue" for seizing them.[14] Downing was released from the Tower in May 1672, after only six weeks, and was once more in favour with the king.

It was undoubtedly Downing's elevation to his post at The Hague – firstly under Cromwell, and then under the king – that put him into a position of power and authority for the rest of his life. On becoming a baronet in 1663, he began to purchase estates in Cambridgeshire, first at East Hatley and later at Bottisham. In 1665 he ceased his role as a diplomat, only to resume it again briefly for the few months back in The Hague in the winter of 1671–2, and then worked for the king in the Treasury. As ever, he quickly rose and was appointed Secretary to the Treasury in 1667, a post that was to bring him substantial rewards. He immediately brought about a change in the way the Treasury operated through the introduction of a new system of internal banking rather than using private bankers as hitherto had been the case. In March 1667 he boastfully showed Pepys chests full of money in the Treasury vaults, as much as £50,000. Bankers were "fearful of Sir G. Downing's being Secretary, he being their enemy", wrote Pepys,[15] who earlier that year had dubbed Downing, reputed as he was for his meanness to those in his employ, "a niggardly fellow".[16] Yet, commenting on Downing's appointment in the Treasury, he declared that: "he is a busy active man, and values himself upon having of things do well under his hand; so that I am mightily pleased in their choice".[17] Only a few months later, in June 1667, Pepys could not refrain from recording that the Exchequer was so full of money it was "ready to break down the floor".[18] Downing, who had been the MP for Dunwich in Suffolk since 1663, and was very active in the House, used his position whenever the chance arose. In 1668 he introduced a Bill into Parliament of which he was very proud, making all the royal revenues assignable directly to the Exchequer and thereby further increasing the flow of money into the coffers. The Lord Chancellor, Lord Clarendon, was rather overshadowed by this action and was suspicious that the only benefit was to line the pockets of Exchequer officials, such as Downing, who is thought to have benefited by as much as £80,000 from the Crown during his various offices.[19]

After his release from the Tower in 1672, Downing was made one of the Commissioners of Customs in London on the substantial salary of £2,000 a year, a post he held for the rest of his life – along with his role as MP for Dunwich – during which time he continued to be a regular contributor to both political and economic matters. In 1666 he had been made Chairman of a Parliamentary Committee for "Advancement of English Manufacturers" and had dabbled in things as diverse as trying to introduce a new plough design from Spain and pottery-making from Holland,[20] showing the ease with which he turned his hand to anything that took his fancy.

Sir George Downing died in 1684, his wife Frances, the first Lady Downing, the year before. In his will he stipulated that he should be interred in the crypt he had made under the chancel of All Saints Church in Croydon, Cambridgeshire (figs. 32-34), along with the body of his spouse. His estate was left to his eldest son, George, and provision also made for his five other children. On his death he was said to be the largest landowner in the shire, the main properties being farms around East Hatley and on the Bedfordshire border. He also owned property at Gamlingay Park, Tadlow, Croydon-cum-Clapton, and in Bedfordshire at Wrestlingworth. By the time the third Sir George Downing inherited the estate twenty-seven years later in 1711, it was 7,000 acres in total.[21]

Although the first Sir George and his lady were prominent landowners in Cambridgeshire – buried in Croydon church with seven other family members added to the tomb in years to come, including the third baronet and founder of the College – no memorial was erected in the church until the College did so in 1961 (fig. 34). It reads: "In a vault beneath the chancel are buried with other members of the Downing family Sir GEORGE DOWNING 1st baronet who died in 1684 and Sir GEORGE DOWNING 3rd baronet, founder of Downing College, Cambridge who died in

32

33

34

35

36

37

32. All Saints Church, Croydon, Cambridgeshire.
33. The Chancel at All Saints Church, under which lies the Downing family tomb.
34. Commemorative plaque to the Downings.
35. St Denis Church, East Hatley, Cambridgeshire.
36 and 37. Arms of Downing impaling those of Howard, in the porch of St Denis Church.

1749."[22] This lack of official acknowledgement to the Downings in the church at Croydon may stem from the fact that Sir George had not had permission to build the vault under the chancel. As H. W. Pettit Stevens put it: "This vault affords another proof of his masterfulness, for he made it without consulting the proper authorities."[23] Pettit Stevens also noted that the baronet had instructed that he should be "buried by the side of his wife in sheep's wooll onely" and that an "affidavit was made of this in accordance with the Act of Parliament of 1666, which he must have helped in passing, the object of the act being to encourage the English woollen trade by lessening the importation of linen from beyond seas".[24] However, there does exist some testimony to the Downing and Howard families in this area of Cambridgeshire – the arms of Downing impaling those of Howard, for Sir George Downing, 1st Baronet and his wife Frances Howard, daughter of Sir William Howard and sister of the 1st Earl of Carlisle – is to be found over the south door of St Denis Church in East Hatley (figs. 35-37), where Sir George purchased his first estate *circa* 1663, less than two miles from the family tomb in the Croydon church and only twelve miles from the College in Cambridge.

The next Sir George Downing, 2nd Baronet (1656–1711), was not the successful man his father had been. Much less is known about him and there is apparently no portrait of him in existence. We do know that in the nepotistic manner of the time this George Downing followed in his father's footsteps as one of the "Tellers of the Exchequer", and that while he married well, to Katherine, eldest daughter of James Cecil, 3rd Earl of Salisbury, it was an unhappy match. The little else that is known about him came to the surface four years after his death during the divorce proceedings in the House of Lords for his son's marriage, when it was stated that he, the father, was "accounted not of sound judgement", and in the local episcopal records of Ely from 1695, it had been stated that he had been "excommunicated for leading an immoral life" with "evidence given by a lay contemporary of an illegitimate son".[25] He was known to be very unkind to his wife, and she died in 1688 leaving the one son, George, born in 1685. There had also been a younger brother, James, who had died in 1686. On the death of his mother, the young George, then three or four years old, was placed in the care of his maternal aunt's family, in the household of Sir William and Lady Forester at Dothill Park near Wellington in Shropshire, and he saw little of his father throughout the rest of his childhood. An agreement to pay for the support of his son's upbringing would clearly have been made between Sir George and the Foresters. To show that he had no plan of disinheriting the boy, he had made a will shortly after his wife's death,

33

leaving the Downing estates to his son, who was thus to become an extremely wealthy man as well as heir to a baronetcy.[26]

This situation within the Downing and Forester families created what was clearly an opportunity not to be missed by the Foresters, who had daughters requiring good marriages. At this time arranged marriages were not uncommon among the noble and wealthier classes for the purposes of gaining financial and social status, the legal age if children were involved being fourteen for a boy and only twelve for a girl. Such marriages, however, required the consent of both sets of parents. It has been surmised that this was not the case here, and that the Foresters made the match between George and their eldest daughter, Mary, without informing Sir George Downing himself.

At this time, the winter of 1699–1700, Sir George was living far away in his manor at East Hatley, with his lover, Priscilla Payne, with whom he is said to have had the illegitimate son. He had already been accused of being of unsound mind and it may have been on these grounds that the Foresters, rather conveniently, felt there was no need to involve him. So the marriage between George and Mary is said to have gone ahead in secret because the Foresters were concerned that, if found out, it would be annulled and they would be accused of being fortune-hunting parents. The Foresters did, however, consider their daughter too young to consummate the marriage, and after the ceremony the newlyweds continued their lives as cousins as if nothing had changed.

George was very soon sent away, it is thought to school initially, and then *circa* 1702 to continental Europe to make the grand tour. Before embarking he begged his young wife, who was said to be a ravishing beauty, that she should decline any invitation to become a Maid of Honour at the new Court of Queen Anne (1702–14), who was known to gather around her the most beautiful ladies of the day. Thus, expecting Mary to sit at home in Shropshire, leading the life of a genteel lady and awaiting her husband's return, George set off to experience the excitement of the Continent, unaware that Sir William and Lady Forester had other ideas for their daughter and were awaiting the command of the Queen that Mary should attend Court. This happened in 1703. At Court she was a great success and became one of the most fashionable and celebrated ladies of the day (fig. 38). Her marriage remained a secret, for only single girls were normally invited to hold such positions. This new and exciting life for Mary continued for many years; she was so popular that she was often to be seen at the queen's side at major events, causing quite a stir in society circles. One such occasion was the first-ever horse race to be held at Ascot in

38

38. Lady (Mary) Downing. Downing College Collection.

39

39. *Sir George Downing, third Baronet and Founder of Downing College. Downing College Collection.*

the summer of 1711, where she was described in the *Globe* newspaper as "a Maid of Honour of remarkable beauty", with particular attention being paid to her apparel: "a small three-cornered cocked hat bound with broad gold lace, a white-powdered long flowing periwig, a cravat tied like a man's, a long white coat, a flapped waistcoat, a flowing skirt being the only variation from the attire of a Cavalier". She can thus be credited with starting this now world-famous English tradition of ladies at Royal Ascot wearing extravagant hats.[27]

Soon after Mary's appointment to Court, the eighteen-year-old George received tidings of this while in Italy. Clearly still in love with his absent spouse, he was heartbroken, and wrote to her saying that he had received letters from mutual friends, "who think they are pleasing me by their lavish description of the beauty and blandishments of my idol". He went on: "I have tried not to believe the story told me . . . do write and say it is not true, and I will once more offer myself to you afresh with a heart more full than your own, or than my own could have heretofore known. I have loved none but you . . . never have I been inconstant for a moment. I can hardly write; by every post I hear something which overpowers me. Write immediately, and do say that you have been faithful."[28] All this pleading achieved nothing, other than a letter back composed by the parents stating the importance of the royal command, with Mary herself defending her own position. George sent a brief reply, stating an end to the matter as far as he was concerned. He then disappeared for a while travelling, arriving back in England in 1704. Ten years then passed with no progress towards any sort of reconciliation between husband and wife, apparently owing in large part to the obstinate character of George. On the death of his father in 1711, he inherited the baronetcy, becoming Sir George Downing, 3rd Baronet (fig. 39). In 1714 Mary petitioned for a divorce, to which George agreed, but the petition was rejected by one vote in the House of Lords, on the grounds that each party had consented to the marriage; the marriage had been properly conducted under Church of England procedure; and there had been no adultery on either side.

In accepting her lot, Mary from then on called herself Dame Mary Downing. Both were locked into an impossible future: "So long as Sir George lived she was condemned to the existence of a married spinster, a wife without a husband; so long as she lived he could father only bastards."[29]

Dame Mary continued her life at Court under the Princess of Wales, the future Queen Caroline, wife of George II, until 1727, when at the age of forty she was retired as a Maid of Honour and spent her remaining years living in Hampton, Middlesex. She died in 1734 and was buried in the vault of Hampton Church. The only items the College possesses to mark this all-important lady are a portrait of her in her younger years now hanging in the Hall, and an ancient inscribed stone from her birthplace, Dothill Park (demolished *circa* 1960), where she had grown up with George, now set into a wall at the west end of the Howard Theatre (fig. 40), which, to quote the eloquent Stanley French, may encourage her ghost to visit Downing, "where she will see the elegant buildings and the spacious lawns of the College which owes its birth to her sterile marriage".[30]

On returning from Italy and before the divorce proceedings, George built himself a mansion on his estate at Gamlingay in Cambridgeshire at a cost of £9,000, and lived there for the rest of his life. His properties now included an estate at Dunwich, where he also spent much of his time. From 1710 he had become MP for that "rotten borough", like his grandfather before him. He was neither a notable MP, making little mark in the House, nor a good landlord or manager; the Downing estates in his time deteriorated markedly. As with his predecessors, he was known to be extremely miserly; he was disliked by his tenants to such a degree that an attempt was made on his life in 1744 and he was nearly killed when a workman attacked him with a hammer and shotgun asserting that "he thought he did no harm by killing a person who paid nobody, and was so ill a landlord and paymaster with so great an estate".[31] In his later years Downing was confined to Gamlingay with severe gout. He had been having a long-term affair with his housekeeper, Mrs Townsend, by whom he had an illegitimate daughter, Elizabeth, born in May 1722.[32] Although his wife had died in 1734, and he lived until 1749, during those intervening fifteen years he did not re-marry or make Elizabeth his legal heir. Elizabeth was, however, well provided for on Sir George's death by a codicil that had been added to his will in 1727.[33] Soon after the unsuccessful divorce proceedings, probably accepting his doomed situation of a childless marriage, Sir George had made his will on 20 December 1717, leaving the Downing estates to four cousins in the following order of inheritance: Jacob Garrard Downing; Thomas Barnardiston; Charles Peters; and John Peters. In the unlikely event that all these beneficiaries should die without heirs, the estate was to form the endowment to create a new college in Cambridge to be called "Downings Colledge".[34] As it happened, they all died childless, and it was upon the death of Jacob Garrard Downing in 1764, the last named heir to die, that the gradual erosion of the Downing fortune began, long before the founding of the College some thirty-six years later.

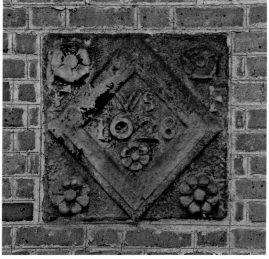

40

40. Stone from Dothill Park, Shropshire, the childhood home of Lady (Mary) Downing (Mary Forester). It is now set into a wall at the west end of the Howard Theatre, Downing College.

41

41. Sir Jacob Garrard Downing, fourth Baronet.
By kind permission of Mr Peter Fullerton.

Death without issue: Lady Margaret Downing and the long litigation

Sir Jacob Garrard Downing (*c.* 1716–1764, fig. 41), also MP for Dunwich, was the only son of Charles Downing, brother of the second baronet. He had been very successful in his own right and was already a wealthy man on inheriting the title. Initially, he improved the estates, which had been badly neglected by his predecessor, and put things in much better order, spending about £30,000 on repairs and new buildings. In 1750 he married Margaret Price, daughter of a Somerset curate who was a graduate of Trinity College, Cambridge, largely on the promise that she would bear him children, which failed to happen. She proved to be a formidable character and as the last Lady Downing took over the management of their joint affairs. Sir Jacob was apparently devoted to her. Perhaps once the reality of yet another childless marriage sank in with this couple, their attitude towards the Downing estates became devious, if not wholly illegal, with regard to the will of the last Sir George. A minor instance of their deviousness was to put any new buildings such as barns on rollers so that in the event of Sir Jacob Downing's death it could be argued that they did not form part of the fixed assets, or else could easily be moved off the estate land. This underhand tactic was nothing compared with Lady Downing's behaviour after the death of her husband in 1764, when her sole aim was to transfer the Downing inheritance to her own family line, regardless of the pre-existing legality of Sir George Downing's will of 1717. The ensuing litigation involved the infamous Court of Chancery where many fortunes were destroyed through years, even decades, of legal battle; the only beneficiaries being the often corrupt lawyers in whose interest it was for cases to be drawn out as much as possible. The lawsuit fought in Chancery between Jarndyce and Jarndyce in Charles Dickens' satirical novel *Bleak House*, resembles something of the way in which Lady (Margaret) Downing, by her determined pursuit of a fortune that was not hers to inherit or pass on, severely depleted the benefaction that had been legally allocated for the founding of Downing College.

When Sir Jacob Downing died in August 1764, his widow, who was his sole executrix, made it quite clear from the outset that she was not prepared to release any of the estates. Apart from the Downing properties he left to his wife, he also left around £100,000 in cash and stocks, as well as another estate with a beautiful house in Putney, London. Even without the Downing inheritance that she also sought to retain, the dowager lady was indeed a very rich widow. Four years after the death of Sir Jacob, in 1768, she re-married, to a naval captain named George Bowyer, but retained her title of Lady Downing. She died at her house in Putney in 1778. Two years before in 1776, one of her last acts on the Downing estates was to tear down the mansion built by the last Sir George as the family seat at Gamlingay Park, selling the contents lot by lot at a fraction of its value. Little wonder that until recently in College circles she was known as "the wicked Lady Downing". Ironically, one of the finest portraits owned by the college, a Gainsborough, showing her in all her splendour (fig. 42), now hangs in the Senior Combination Room for the pleasure of the Fellowship. Previously this portrait, unknown as a Gainsborough, had hung in the dining-hall for many years and was the favoured target of undergraduate food missiles.

Margaret Bowyer as the last Lady Downing was buried in the family vault under the chancel of All Saints Church in Croydon, Cambridgeshire, alongside the baronets whose family fortune she had attempted to steal. Even from beyond the grave she fought on with plans put in place long before her death: in her will of December 1772, she had made sure that after she was gone the fight against the foundation of Downing College would continue, which is what caused the long legal battle and the loss of most of the benefaction for the creation of the College. She divided her estate between her second husband, to whom she left all her Downing properties in the county of Suffolk, and many other relatives, including a niece named Diana Say who was to receive "all my houses in Downing Street, Westminster", also valuable Downing estate property. But the main benefactor was her nephew, Jacob John Whittington, an army officer, whom she appointed her sole executor and to whom she left "all my landed estates in the counties of Cambridgeshire and Bedfordshire to him and to his heirs forever", which amounted to the bulk of the Downing estate. This was a slap in the face to the heirs-at-law of the third Sir George Downing and the Masters and Scholars of the University of Cambridge, who now had a daunting fight on their hands if they were to realise the creation of the new college.

The heirs-at-law representing the third baronet's wishes were six ladies who had all inherited this role from their predecessors: two grand-daughters and four great grand-daughters of the first Sir George Downing. These were all genteel ladies with neither the skill nor the wherewithal required to fight such legal action against Dowager Lady Downing. Even after her death they were confronted with the formidable opposition from those who stood to gain so substantially from this final and illicit will of the "wicked Lady". At this point, around 1778–9, a champion for the Downing cause appeared on the scene: an MP named Francis Annesley. As the son of Mary Annesley, one of the heirs-at-law and great-grandson of the first Sir George,

42

42. *Lady (Margaret) Downing. Downing College Collection.*

43

43. *Francis Annesley, first Master of Downing College. Downing College Collection.*

he had Downing blood in his veins. Francis Annesley (fig. 43) was to play a major, defining role in the legal battle and before long was being referred to as the "Master of Downing".[35] Years of further complex legal wrangling through the Court of Chancery ensued with the heirs-at-law headed by Annesley, along with representatives of the University, fighting against George Bowyer and John Jacob Whittington, the widowed husband and the executor nephew, both the biggest beneficiaries under Dowager Lady Downing's will. The long battle drew much attention within society circles, appeals were made to King George, with several petitions being presented and failing, until at last, on 22 September 1800, the charter for the founding of the College was granted.

Homeless: the first Master and Fellows

Though the legal battle had been won, and the 1717 will of the third Sir George Downing at last honoured – eighty-three years after it had been written, and fifty-one years after his death – a fraction of the original estate remained for the funding of the College at just under £10,000, or some £9 million in today's money.[36] During the lawsuit several sites for the College in Cambridge had been considered, mainly to give the case some practical viability in the eyes of the Court and to show that the executors were in earnest. As early as 1772 a site lying between and to the south of Pembroke and Emmanuel Colleges had been identified, and the local architect, James Essex, had been involved in drawing up plans for negotiation of the land. This site, known as Pembroke Leys, was to be the eventual site of the College, but at this point the purchase had failed and other sites had been sought, simply to encourage and satisfy the Court, irrespective of their practicality for building a college on. A site of just under two acres had been identified at Pound Hill, on the north edge of the city centre; and a much larger site of about fifteen acres on what is now Parker's Piece, just to the east of the College site today. Purchase of these sites had also failed, and in 1798 the executors in their frustration purchased a tiny site of less than an acre on the southern edge of Midsummer Common named Dolls Close, which proved sufficient to convince the Court of Chancery that they were determined in their drive to build the College. Even though this totally inadequate site was quite impractical, as Bowyer and Whittington were at pains to point out, they were overruled by the Court who accepted the intention of Annesley and his associates, at last showing some sympathy with the Downing cause. Very shortly after this, the Court gave the heirs-at-law permission to renew their application for a charter, at which point they needed to establish a governing body and the first list of the small Fellowship was drawn up:

Frances Annesley, Master; Busick Harwood, Downing Professor of Medicine; Edward Christian, Downing Professor of the Laws of England; John Lens, William Meek and William Frere, Fellows. Though there was continued objection from Bowyer, Whittington and their powerful supporters, the king had by now become weary of the endless legal arguments and pushed the case forward. This was a major achievement for Annesley who, having matriculated from St John's College at Easter 1800 by special mandate from the king, was admitted to the higher degree of Doctor of Civil Law on 24 May: "Never before or since has a degree conferred without examination been so strenuously earned."[37]

The terms of the new College's charter and statutes were radical and modern in that they were designed, so wrote Stanley French, "to keep Downing College free from the anachronistic restrictions, myopic outlook and sloth-inducing atmosphere of the older foundations". He went on to say: "It was to be a perpetual College for students in 'Law, physic and the other useful arts and learning'. To prevent the ossification apparent elsewhere only the Master, the Professors and two clerical Fellows were to hold office for life; the rest of the Fellowship were limited to a tenure of twelve years whilst their holders were 'going forward' in their chosen professions". Furthermore, he added: "The allocation of only two Fellowships to men in Holy Orders would ensure that Downing would not be a predominantly clerical society like other colleges." This last point largely did away with the celibacy rule for fellows so common in Oxbridge colleges of the past whereby they would have to forfeit their fellowships on getting married. Annesley, as Master, was central in drawing up the College statutes, and it was his intention at Downing "to supply whatever is defective in the ancient establishments". As French, writing further about Annesley, stated: "He wanted Downing to begin and to remain free from the clerical domination, unworldly seclusion, toleration of idleness, neglect of scholarship, ineffective use of resources and absence of purpose which to a greater or lesser degree afflicted the old foundations of both Oxford and Cambridge . . . Downing was intended to stand as a shining example of what a nineteenth-century [i.e. modern] college should be."[38]

The College now existed in name and fellowship, but there was as yet no physical home for its members to occupy. The task to find a suitable and affordable site was now taken up by Annesley along with Edward Christian, the Professor of Law and brother of Fletcher Christian who, just over a decade earlier in 1789, had led the mutiny on HMS *Bounty*. Going full circle on previous explorations for a site for the College, the originally preferred site of Pembroke Leys at over thirty acres was again chosen as the most suitable. However, this was a complex purchase involving many owners, tenants and holders of common pasture rights, and it did not become possible to complete the sale until 1807 at a cost of just under £5,500. Now they were to have a site on which to build, it was time to find an architect to design the first new college in Cambridge for more than 200 years.

Notes
1 French, p. 7.
2 Simmons, p. 4.
3 Ibid.
4 A present-day descendent of John Winthrop is John Kerry, another Governor of Massachusetts, and US Secretary of State.
5 Pettit Stevens, p. 8 and Shallard, p. 119.
6 Pettit Stevens, p. 9.
7 Ibid., p. 12.
8 Shallard, p. 124.
9 Ibid., p. 125.
10 Evelyn, 12 July 1666, quoted in Pettit Stevens, p.17.
11 Bolitho, p. 20.
12 Sir John Major on "The One Show" BBC 1, 14 July 2014.
13 Pepys, 12 March 1662, quoted in Shallard, p. 127.
14 Pepys, 12 March 1662, quoted in Pettit Stevens, p.17.
15 Pepys, 28 May 1667.
16 Pepys, 27 February 1667, quoted in Shallard, p. 129.
17 Pepys, 27 May 1667, quoted in Shallard, p. 129.
18 Pepys, 14 June 1667, quoted in Shallard, p. 129.
19 Pettit Stevens, p. 17.
20 Shallard, p. 130.
21 Henderson, p. 19.
22 Shallard, p. 132.
23 Pettit Stevens, p. 18.
24 Ibid.
25 Pettit Stevens, p. 19.
26 French, pp. 7 and 8.
27 Ibid., p. 16.
28 Pettit Stevens, pp. 23–4.
29 French, p. 26.
30 Ibid., p. 30.
31 Pettit Stevens, p. 30.
32 French, p. 37.
33 Ibid., pp 36, 37 and 45.
34 Pettit Stevens, pp. 37–8.
35 French, p. 68.
36 Henderson, p. 20.
37 French, p. 81.
38 Ibid., pp. 82–4.

F. Mackenzie.

J. Le Keux.

DOWNING COLLEGE,

AS IT WILL APPEAR WHEN COMPLETED.

44

42

3 Concepts and ideas: the competition to build Downing's College

William Wilkins' concept for the design of Downing College in 1805 was superbly inventive and innovative at a point in the history of architecture – and in the history of collegiate planning in Cambridge – that was both thrilling andrefreshing. His plan marked a radical move away from the traditional monastic layout of Oxbridge colleges, and his choice at this time of the neo-Greek style, as opposed to the exhausted neo-classical of the period or the neo-Gothic that was fermenting in the wings, was to define this new Cambridge college as something different and special. Unfortunately, the full plan was never executed, and although today one can get a feel of the original concept immediately upon entering the vast expanse of the main court (see frontispiece or fig. 207, p. 194), the College of today is only a shadow of what could have been. Had it been fully built, Downing would undoubtedly have been one of the most important examples anywhere of a neo-classical composition in the Greek Revival style. In plan alone, it was the forerunner of the American campus universities, pre-empting Thomas Jefferson's University of Virginia by ten years.

The design and building of Downing College was an event that would inevitably attract a lot of attention, but the process was not straightforward. Although seven architects in total were involved, no formal competition took place. The protracted legal battle fought through Chancery in the last three decades of the eighteenth century had a profound bearing on the design and building stages, creating an unusual and problematic relationship between the architects involved and the somewhat nebulous "client". In fact, there was no identifiable client for many years, as neither the College as a physical entity, nor a fellowship as a tangible group of people, existed, all matters being controlled by the Court and through numerous committees. For any architect pursuing this exciting and prestigious commission in the early years, it must have been awkward and frustrating owing to the lack of client instruction and a proper brief. What was particularly unusual was to design a whole college from scratch without a proper client to provide guidance and without anything to establish a precedent. There was a precedent, to be sure, in the form of the older and overwhelmingly medieval colleges with their monastic plans and Gothic-style buildings. However, in 1784 the king, George III, had requested that the design of the new College should be in the classical style, not Gothic.[1] The obvious precedent had thus been rejected by royal command.

44. The south range of Downing College as intended, with the Hall in the foreground, and Master's Lodge in the distance (both completed), and the unbuilt Library and Chapel in the centre. By J. Le Keux after F. Mackenzie, 1842. Downing College Archive.

The first official architect for Downing College was James Essex, appointed in 1771. As Michael Tyson, a Fellow of Corpus Christi College, wrote to Richard Gough, Secretary of the Society of Antiquaries, in a letter from that year: "Essex is come down from London with a commission to purchase, at any rate, Pembroke Leas, to build Downing College upon, and immediately to draw a plan and elevation of the new College. The charter is to be framed out of hand, and the foundation laid as soon as possible."[2] This initial attempt of the heirs-at-law of the third Sir George Downing to purchase this very desirable site on the outskirts of Cambridge for the College was unsuccessful at this time, as we have seen, but as no drawings have survived, it is not known if Essex took the project any further before his death in 1784. Nevertheless, he may well have done so, and in the Gothic style, which could explain the king's anti-Gothic intervention at such an early stage in the proceedings.[3]

The situation with regard to lack of client participation improved only with the granting of the foundation charter in 1800 when a small Fellowship, or Governing Body, was at last formed. However, this body of men comprising fellows of other Cambridge colleges, alongside individuals from London, such as Dr Annesley, the newly appointed first Master, had not yet had time to develop collectively any sense of what form their new College should take, other than it should be classical at the king's behest. Furthermore, after the failure to secure Pembroke Leys, any architect involved would be designing site-less and, unconstrained by brief or site, creative flare would be free to run wild.

Soon after the death of Essex, James Wyatt, the next architect of the College, appeared on the scene in the company of Annesley. Mr Michael Lort, a Fellow of Trinity College, recorded their visit in a letter dated 27 October 1784: "Mr Ainsly [sic] the new Master of Downing has been here to fix on a site for his new College, for, though many has been proposed to him, yet objections are made to all – Mr Wyat [sic] the architect wishes much that it should be opposite to some of the colleges on the River, for then he thinks he shall not be crampt for Room, & may make four fine facades; but how will they here get an access to, & communication with, the Town? The most promising spot seems to be that between Bp Watsons house and the Tennis Court, but there tis said they cannot dig cellars, a material object, I presume, to such a college."[4]

45

45. Plan of Pembroke Leys, 1803, the future site of the College. Downing College Archive.

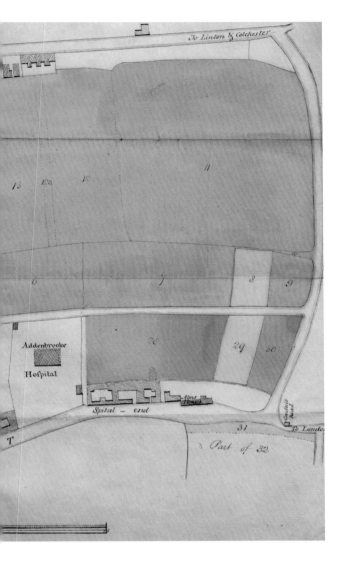

Monumental indulgence along the Backs – James Wyatt

James Wyatt (1746–1813) was the most celebrated and highly sought-after architect of the period, who had already worked in Oxford and was thus experienced with university clients. It is interesting that Wyatt should have had his eye on building along the river opposite some of the ancient colleges on the water meadows of the west bank, unsuitable for basements or cellars. At this early stage of Wyatt's involvement, which would span the following twenty years, the College still had not found any other sites to build on after the unsuccessful attempt to purchase Pembroke Leys. It is therefore curious that the scheme proposed by Wyatt in 1804 (figs. 46-48) was so massive in scale and clearly only viable for a very large site. It is conjectured that the date of Wyatt's scheme may go back to his initial involvement in 1784, at which time these would have been drawings in the air for a site somewhere along the Backs, an area that would not be built on for another forty-one years, until St John's College created the neo-Gothic New Court by Rickman and Hutchinson in 1825–31. That this idea may have been in Wyatt's mind is not surprising, as he would have been aware of Lancelot "Capability" Brown's scheme of five years earlier in 1779, proposing a major re-planning of the Backs. Brown's idea was that all the individual colleges in the area would give up their boundary rights and agree to the creation of a typically Brownian park stretching uninterruptedly from Queens' College in the south to St John's in the north. It was a wonderful concept that was never to materialise; but what an amazing location for Downing or indeed any college this would have been! However, when attention again reverted to Pembroke Leys in 1801 and the future acquisition of that site at last became a reality, all subsequent designs for the College were based on it, including Wyatt's, which would fit comfortably on the expansive thirty acres (fig. 45).

By the early 1800s the College had thus secured the purchase of its site and had an impressive scheme by the leading architect of the day. On submitting his designs for approval early in 1804, Wyatt also provided a report that gave a list of the accommodation to be provided. The wording for this may have been taken from the founding charter, effectively acting as a brief: "space required to accommodate a Master – Two Professors – Sixteen Fellows and from sixteen to twenty Undergraduates; with a Chapel, Library and Hall; Bursery [sic], Muniment Room, Common Room Etc, Etc."[5] He estimated the construction cost to be a minimum of £60,000. At this point, however, Frances Annesley took the extraordinary step of seeking a second opinion of the scheme. He may not have been impressed with Wyatt's somewhat stale and soon-to-become outmoded neo-classicism, especially if his drawings were indeed twenty years old. He sent Wyatt's drawings to a leading expert of the day, Thomas Hope (1769–1831). A rich connoisseur, patron of the arts and member of the Society of Dilettanti, Hope was, like many intellectuals at the time, passionate about all things Greek. In a letter back to Annesley dated 22 February 1804, Hope proceeded to destroy Wyatt's Roman Doric proposal with the most severe criticism and promoted a Grecian alternative, stating that he wished that "instead of the degraded architecture of the Romans, the purest style of the Greeks had been exclusively adhibited". He pulled apart Wyatt's designs in detail, concluding that he could not see "one striking feature, one eminent beauty. Neither elevations nor sections display a single instance of fancy, a single spark of genius, to make up for their many faults. Every thing [*sic*] alike in them is trite, common place, nay, often vulgar."[6] To make matters worse, Hope published the letter as a pamphlet entitled *Observations on the Plans and Elevations Designed by James Wyatt, Architect, for Downing College, Cambridge; in a Letter to Francis Annesley, Esq., M.P.* The whole episode caused uproar and Wyatt, who was then President of the Royal Academy, had Hope barred from the annual dinner, though Hope's cause was promoted by Sir John Soane, architect and professor at the Academy, and an apology was later granted. All this was Hope's cunning way of championing his protégé, Wilkins, recently home from a grand tour of the Mediterranean, and positioning him for the Downing commission.

In this turbulent period of debate about style, powerful intellectual forces were at work not only in the capital, but in the University too, which would soon start to dictate the fresh choice of an architect. At Cambridge, a group of scholars known as the Hellenists or Graecophils, especially concentrated in colleges such as Trinity and St John's and soon to include such prominent figures as Lord Byron, were strong advocates of the Greek Revival and about to join the fray to ensure the success of their candidates. One should not forget that this was the time when Thomas Bruce, 7th Earl of Elgin, between 1801 and 1812, removed many marble sculptures from the temple of the Parthenon on the Acropolis in Athens and transported them back to the British Museum; such was the passion then for Greek antiquity.

Annesley's action inviting Hope's intervention at this point brought proceedings to a halt. The Master of the Court of Chancery requested that a second scheme with costs should be sought. In the eyes of the Graecophils this delay had the desired effect; it created time to position Wilkins while he prepared his own ideas for the

46-48: the designs of James Wyatt for Downing College. RIBA Library Drawings and Archives Collections.

46

47

48

design of the College. In the meantime, the alternative scheme requested by the Court was set in train.

Sophisticated neo-classical elegance – George Byfield

The architect invited to submit this next proposal was George Byfield (c. 1756–1813), known mainly for his design of county gaols, including that at Cambridge, which he was building at that time (1802–7, demolished 1930), and the Suffolk County Gaol of 1803 at nearby Bury St Edmunds. Though nothing like as fashionable as Wyatt, Byfield ran a successful practice in London, where he was estates surveyor for the Dean and Chapter of Westminster. He also built several elegant country houses with interiors in the Adam fashion, dallied with Gothick at Brockhampton Chapel in Herefordshire, and with Greek Revival in his Sessions House (now part of Canterbury Christ Church University) at Canterbury, where he also built the gaol in 1806–10.[7] He had also worked for an influential local Cambridge family, the Yorkes, Earls of Hardwicke, whose family seat was at Wimpole Hall, a few miles south-west of the city. Through this connection there was contact with a number of leading Cambridge academics such as Dr Craven, the Master of St John's College, and Edward Christian, the first Downing Professor of the Laws of England.[8] As he was already active in the area, Byfield had well-established working relationships with local craftsmen and was ideally placed to provide the Master of the Court with competitive tenders to compete with Wyatt's. He was thus championed by this new Cambridge faction, who saw an opportunity for him to succeed as its architect for the Downing commission.

Byfield's design for Downing (figs. 49–51) was detailed and thorough. His large three-sided court open to the south as a shallow U-shaped plan, was remarkably similar in layout to that of the College court today: a wide north range of six hundred feet across with the chapel at its centre, and ranges to east and west projecting south. So convincing was his design that by February 1805 he had successfully wrested the commission from Wyatt and was in a strong position to succeed.

In April 1805 Byfield exhibited his drawings at the Royal Academy annual exhibition, to be surprisingly joined by Wilkins, who, for the first time, presented his designs for the College. Competition was mounting. Possibly owing to the stir Byfield had caused by the ousting of Wyatt, within the year three more architects joined the fray: Francis Sandys, an Irish architect; William Porden; and then Lewis William

49–51: the designs of George Byfield for Downing College. Downing College Archive.

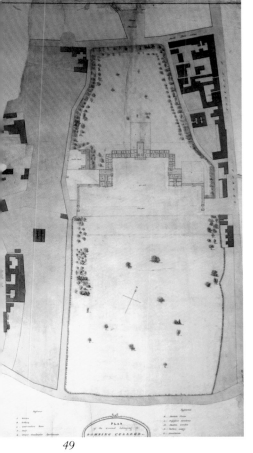

49

ELEVATION of the MASTERS HOUSE and END of the WEST WING

50

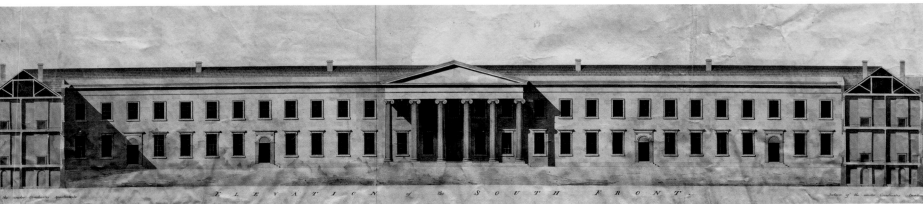

ELEVATION of the SOUTH FRONT

51

Wyatt, the nephew of James Wyatt, each with a new scheme. This was an extraordinary development as no official competition had been announced, and there had been little attention paid to it in the national press. Yet, in London and Cambridge cultural circles the Downing project had become a great aesthetic issue arousing heated debate and controversy, with the race to choose an architect becoming a *cause célèbre* of British architecture. None of Sandys' drawings have survived, but as the architect of Ickworth House near Bury St Edmunds, his proposal would have undoubtedly been competent and interesting. So, by spring 1806 there were three more new schemes for the design of the College, all of them fascinating in their own right, and one in particular which must have been a shock.

A spectacular Gothic palace in a romantic landscape – William Porden

William Porden (*c*.1755–1822) submitted the most extraordinary Gothic design for Downing that flew in the face of all the rules that had been established for the project (figs. 52-56). He must surely have been aware that his actions were deliberately in defiance of the king, the neo-classicists and the Graecophils. Porden had formerly been a pupil of James Wyatt, which, of course, would not have gone in his favour in pursuing the Downing commission, but by this time he had established himself as a leading Gothic architect, concurrently employed by the Prince Regent on minor works at the Brighton Pavilion (1804–8), and also designing one of the most extravagant Gothic houses of the period, Eaton Hall in Cheshire (1804–12).

Porden's approach to the planning of the new College – particularly the placing of the composition within the context of the Pembroke Leys site and its overall landscaping – was undoubtedly one of the most creative of all the schemes put forward, even if the style of architecture was considered inappropriate and unacceptable. In order to maximise the impact of the site in his overall concept, he placed his buildings further north than in any of the other architects' schemes, thus leaving a large area of open space to the south (fig. 52). Though overwhelmingly Gothic, the buildings did not consist of enclosed courtyards in the monastic tradition. Rather, it was an open and spacious layout that responded beautifully to the site, whereby a central core of main buildings – chapel, hall and library – was contained by flanking residential ranges to east and west, with the continuous space of the long site invited to flow both around and between those component parts and to continue uninterrupted from south to north, or *vice versa* (fig. 52). Entrance to the site was from the north and south ends, though the most dramatic way to approach the College would have been from the

52 and 53: William Porden's block site plan and landscaping plan. RIBA Library Drawings and Archives Collections.

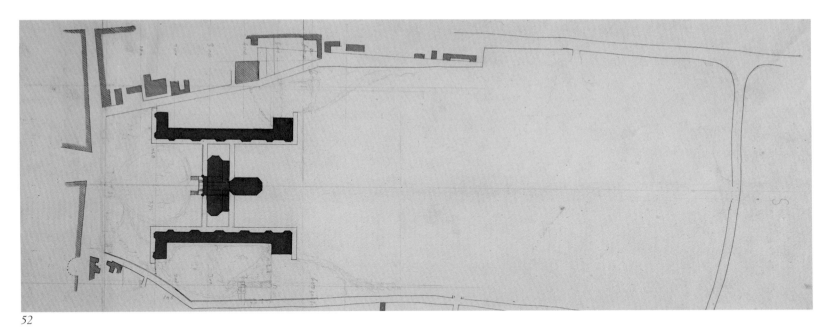

52

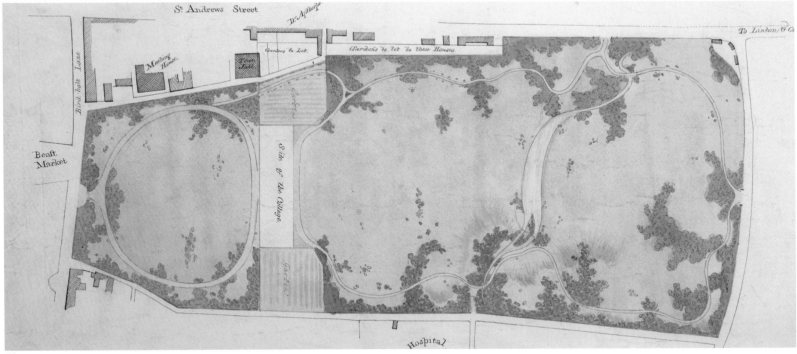

53

longer route in the south through a landscaped park creating an atmosphere of pastoral tranquillity (fig. 53). Meandering lanes ran up both perimeters of the site, to east and west, through strategically planted tree formations, so that on horseback or by carriage one would get teasing glimpses of the distant buildings until the surprise of the astounding architectural scene to the north was finally revealed. Half way up the site, a gently winding stream crossed from west to east bulging to form a lake, thus providing the essential element of water to complete the experience. The whole effect of this pastoral setting and the allusion to something wonderful ahead suggested classical rather than medieval associations; the last thing one would expect to find at the end of this journey would have been a massive Gothic pile. In Cinzia Sicca's assessment, "Porden's design was as much representative of the aesthetic issues of his times as the neo-classical projects submitted by Byfield and Wilkins." She went on to say: "Gothic was a style which could be described and was perceived as a native one, embodying the spirit of association and the community of national feeling . . . Although generally dismissed as a 'fluke' in previous accounts of the architectural history of the college, Porden's design should be recognised as one of the most carefully thought out projects submitted to the attention of the Fellowship and the most serious challenger, both intellectually and architecturally, of Wilkins' Greek design."[9]

By December 1805 the Fellowship had considered and rejected the schemes of Byfield, Sandys and Porden, and it was looking very likely that Wilkins was about to be declared the architect of the College. However, much to the Graecophils' surprise, Lewis William Wyatt submitted a scheme that had the powerful backing of several of the heirs-at-law of Sir George Downing, meaning that it had to be seriously considered by the College and the Court of Chancery. Just before Christmas, the Master of the Court assessed the situation and both Wilkins and Lewis William Wyatt were requested to make adjustments to their schemes, thus causing further delay. This must have been a frustrating development for both Wilkins and the Graecophils, who had momentarily thought they were home and dry. They were now faced with another serious contender, who not only had the substantial support of a legitimate faction representing the will of the founder, but a new and impressive design to compete with that of Wilkins.

54-6: William Porden's designs for Downing College. RIBA Library Drawings and Archives Collections.

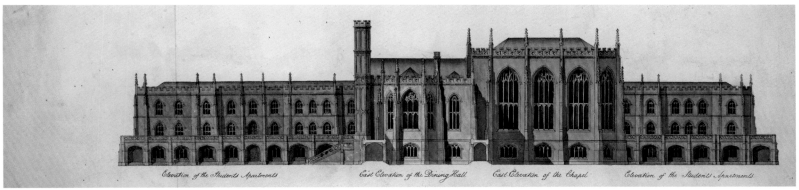

Elevation of the Students Apartments   *East Elevation of the Dining Hall*   *East Elevation of the Chapel*   *Elevation of the Students Apartments*

54

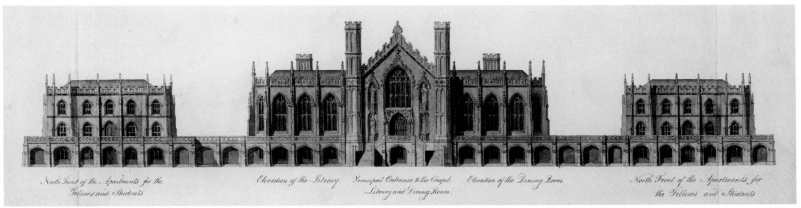

North Front of the Apartments for the Fellows and Students   *Elevation of the Library*   *Principal Entrance to the Chapel Library and Dining Room*   *Elevation of the Dining Room*   *North Front of the Apartments for the Fellows and Students*

55

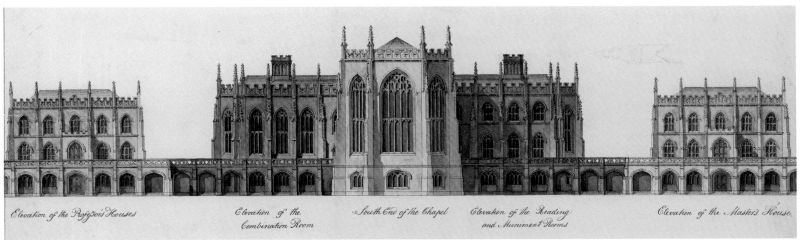

Elevation of the Professors Houses   *Elevation of the Combination Room*   *South End of the Chapel*   *Elevation of the Reading and Muniment Rooms*   *Elevation of the Master's House*

56

A fashionable city residence – Lewis William Wyatt

A member of the Wyatt dynasty of architects, who had been prominent throughout the eighteenth and well into the nineteenth century, Lewis William Wyatt (1777–1853) was the nephew of and former apprentice to James Wyatt, the second architect for Downing, whose scheme had been so savaged by Hope in 1804. One can assume that Wyatt's intention was not only fuelled by his own wish to succeed, but also to some degree by a desire to restore the family honour and regain this prestigious commission lost by his uncle. Like Wilkins, Lewis Wyatt was a young architect just starting out on his own who had not yet handled a large commission. Wyatt's approach was along similar neo-classical lines to his uncle's, but with a fresher and more contemporary handling of the composition and the orders in such a way that could not be criticised as being the stale neo-classical style of the recent past (figs. 58–60).

As with those of both Wilkins and Wyatt's uncle, his plan was a large quadrangle similarly placed towards the middle of the site (fig. 57), and accessed from Bird Bolt Lane in the north (now Pembroke/Downing Streets). Again, as with Wilkins' plan, the entrance proceeded down an avenue towards the gateway into the College, which was flanked to east and west by an enclosed colonnade to the north side, open on the court side to the south and terminating at either end by square accommodation blocks. Another similarity to Wilkins' plan was the south range of Wyatt's composition, which consisted of the main buildings of the College – the library, chapel and hall – and like the north range again connected to square blocks to east and west: that to the east containing the Master's Lodge, as in most of the schemes; and the west block the common room, kitchens and offices. The free-standing east and west ranges were not joined to the north and south; each consisted of a main, central block as self-contained houses for the two Professors, flanked on either side by residential buildings for Fellows in the west range, and undergraduates in the east. On the east side of the east range towards the street, there was to be another entrance into a crescent-shaped drive with a planted elliptical island, from which there was private access to the Master's Lodge to the south. In many areas, the planning of the young Wyatt's composition was highly reminiscent of Wilkins' design, though it is interesting that Wilkins during his adjustments requested by the Court, also copied Wyatt's idea of separating the two Professors' houses to east and west, as opposed to his initial scheme where they were both on the east side. Here, Wyatt went one step further in his separation, too, of the Fellows' and students' accommodation on opposite sides of the quadrangle,

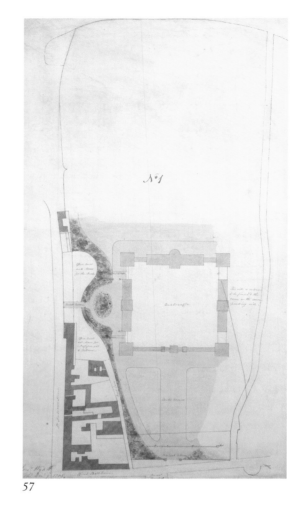

57

57–60: Lewis William Wyatt's designs (Downing College Archive):

57. Site Plan of 1805.

58. Elevation of the East Range, with sections through a triumphal entrance arch and chapel.

59. Elevation of the south front of the North Range.

60. Elevation of the principal South Range.

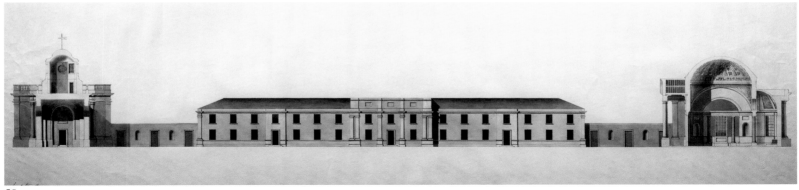

58

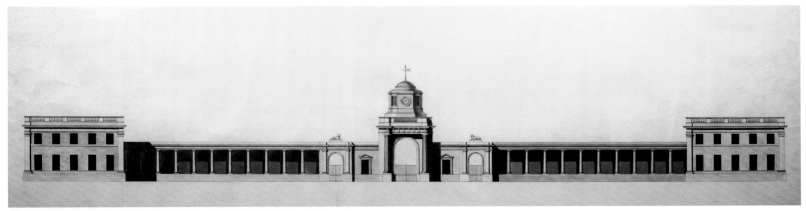

59

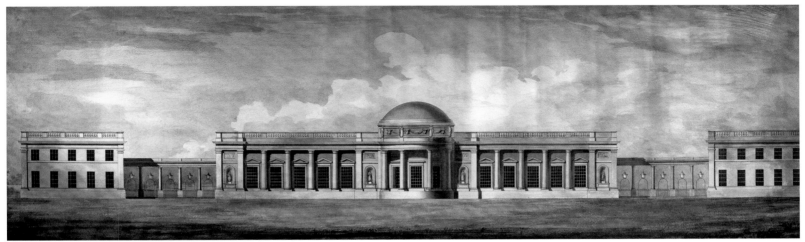

60

placing one Professor and all the Fellows on the west side, and the Master, a Professor and all the students on the east. With regard to architectural statement and presence, again, as with Wilkins' plan, the most striking of Wyatt's elevations were the north range with the entrance gate, and both elevations of the main south range, with the residential east and west ranges being comparatively plain and domestic in character.

The introduction of Wyatt's scheme at this point in late 1805 caused a temporary deadlock in proceedings, and it was not until March 1806 that things began to move again when the Master of the Court decided that the only solution was to seek the professional opinion of three respected architects to choose between the two designs. Both Wilkins and Lewis Wyatt were consulted and the three architects chosen as judges were: Samuel Pepys Cockerell (1753–1827), George Dance the younger (1741–1825), and James Lewis (c.1751–1820), all of whom were prominent neo-classical architects with an understanding of exactly what was before them. The Master of the Court, Francis Stratford, had instructed the panel to comment on technical as well as aesthetic grounds. Both schemes were deemed technically of equal competence, though not without criticism and with adjustment being required. However, in the final decision it inevitably came down to aesthetic preferences. With the ever-growing trend towards the Greek Revival of the time, Wilkins was clearly in an advantageous position over Wyatt and emerged victorious. The judges' report of 26 March 1806 was categorical: "The distribution of the several principal parts in each design are somewhat similar but the details of the plan very superior in that of Mr Wilkins . . . The general decorations of Mr Wilkins design adopted from Grecian models possess more grandeur simplicity and classical effect than those of Mr L. Wyatt."[10] Though they were complimentary to Wilkins about his overall concept and mastery of the Greek idiom, the judges were also unanimously critical on several counts, especially to do with the young architect's apparent failure to relate elevation to plan, the inadequate internal layout of the Master's Lodge and the Professors' houses being particularly noted. There was another major criticism: "We are apprehensive that the unpleasant communication between the Kitchen and the Hall or Refectory by a winding subterraneous passage of 140 feet in length from which its termination everything must be brought up steps exposed to all Weathers thro the floor of the portico of the Refectory will prove very inconvenient and objectionable and in some measure degrade the appearance of the portico itself."[11] However, with all these perfectly correctable points noted, Wilkins had at last won the commission and was clear to proceed with his design for the new College.

Classical purity from the ancient world – William Wilkins

61

61. Bust of William Wilkins in the Hall corridor. Downing College Collection.

Given that William Wilkins (1778–1839, fig. 61) had very little experience as a practical architect before the submission of his designs for Downing College in 1805, his achievement is all the more extraordinary. At the same time he also won the competition to design the new East India College in Hertfordshire, now Haileybury School. As we have seen, Wilkins was the son of a builder and self-taught architect, and had been educated at Norwich Grammar School, whence he proceeded, on a scholarship, to Gonville and Caius College, Cambridge, in 1796 to read mathematics, graduating BA in 1800. During his time as an undergraduate, his interest in architecture intensified, presumably inspired by his surroundings, living in the heart of Cambridge; he made a study of King's College Chapel, producing a set of measured drawings showing great talent as a natural draughtsman (now housed in Columbia University, New York City). He also exhibited two drawings at the Royal Academy annual exhibition in 1799, one being a study of the Gate of Honour at his own college, one of the earliest classical structures in Cambridge designed by Dr Caius in the sixteenth century (see fig. 15, p. 19). Wilkins had thus come to prominence at a young age, and soon after graduation was promoted by various established academics, including Sir Busick Harwood, the first Downing Professor of Medicine, to membership of the prestigious Society of Antiquaries. A year later in 1801 he left England to make his grand tour to study the ancient architecture of the Mediterranean countries, returning home in the summer of 1803. It was from these years abroad that he acquired his knowledge of classical architecture. The inspiration for the design of both Downing and Haileybury came from a scholarly study of the ancient buildings of such places as Athens. At this time, it was rare for anyone to have such a first-hand knowledge of Greek architecture, and Wilkins would have been hailed as a leading expert in the field. Upon his return to Cambridge he was made a Junior Fellow of his College, and at about that time, possibly through Harwood, became a member of the Cambridge Hellenists or Graecophils, leading to his association with Thomas Hope and the possible conspiracy to bring about the downfall of James Wyatt as the prospective architect of Downing.

It was Wilkins' interpretation of Greek style, and his innovatory composition for the planning of Downing, that clearly won him the approval of the three judges in March 1806, notwithstanding the technical problems they had brought to light, which took several months to resolve. His original drawings have not survived, nor has the revised set showing the improvements he submitted in June 1806, so it is not possible to see the faults that had been outlined by his older superiors, or how he rectified them. Nevertheless the judges provided a report, which gave a detailed description of what Wilkins' proposal consisted of at this stage: "The general form would be a quadrangle comprehending an area 350 feet long by 214 feet whereof the Southern Division would exhibit the principal front of Grecian architecture of the Ionic Order and would contain a Library 60 feet long by 30 feet wide a Chapel 70 feet long by 20 feet wide. The Northern Division would contain a Grand Entrance from the Town of Grecian Architecture of the Doric Order with Porters Lodges and apartments for 8 Fellows and 10 Undergraduates. The Eastern Division would contain the Public Kitchens & Offices, Lodges for the 2 professors with the necessary Offices & apartments for 4 Fellows and 4 Undergraduates and the Western Division would contain a Lecture Room 24 feet long by 19 feet wide a Lodge for the Master with the necessary Offices and apartments for 4 Fellows 2 Chaplains and 6 Undergraduates comprising in the whole Accommodation for the Master 2 Professors 16 Fellows 2 Chaplains & 20 Undergraduates as directed by the said Orders."[12]

On 31 July 1806 the Court of Chancery approved Wilkins as architect, and fifty-seven years after the death of the third Sir George Downing, the Master and Fellows were at last given the go-ahead to build their College. This was not just a personal triumph for Wilkins, but one for all those behind the Downing cause, such as Francis Annesley and the heirs-at-law, who had fought tirelessly to reach this point. It was a success particularly for the Graecophils in the University, who were at long last going to fulfil their dream of building a whole new college as an Athenian monument on the edge of medieval Cambridge: an incredible statement of radical change reflecting the start of a new era in college building and marking the beginning of the modern university.

Inspired by the example of the antique agora from ancient Greece and the Forum from Rome, Wilkins changed fundamentally the way a courtyard or quadrangular space had traditionally been laid out by replacing continuous ranges with a looser composition of individual buildings, freer in approach but still achieving a sense of enclosure. His idea clearly caught the imagination of the three judges leading to their approval of this new vision. Placed midway down the long Pembroke Leys site (fig. 64), the composition (figs. 62–75) consisted of twelve individual pavilions connected by screen walls, though the main range to the south, containing the Chapel and Library, was totally free-standing but set on a defined podium of three steps linking it at base level to the flanking east and west ranges. The approach to the College was from Bird Bolt Lane in the north (now Downing Street), along a 300-yard avenue through a park

62. Early block plan of the College by William Wilkins. Downing College Archive.

63. Elevation of the intended South Range buildings. Though both of these drawings show the podium platform linking the South Range buildings, this was not consistently present on later drawings. Downing College Collection.

63

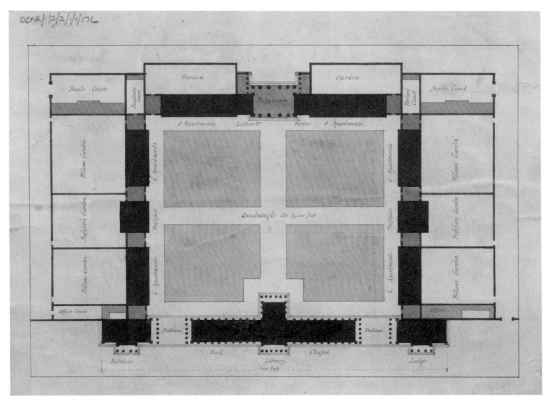

62

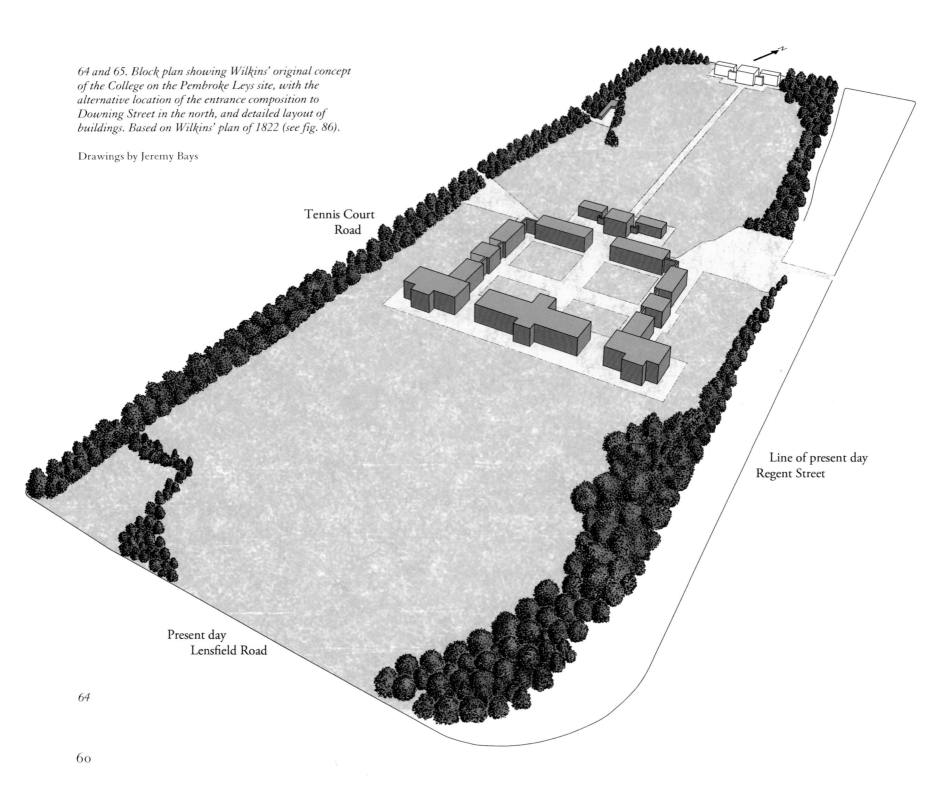

64 and 65. Block plan showing Wilkins' original concept of the College on the Pembroke Leys site, with the alternative location of the entrance composition to Downing Street in the north, and detailed layout of buildings. Based on Wilkins' plan of 1822 (see fig. 86).

Drawings by Jeremy Bays

Tennis Court
Road

Line of present day
Regent Street

Present day
Lensfield Road

64

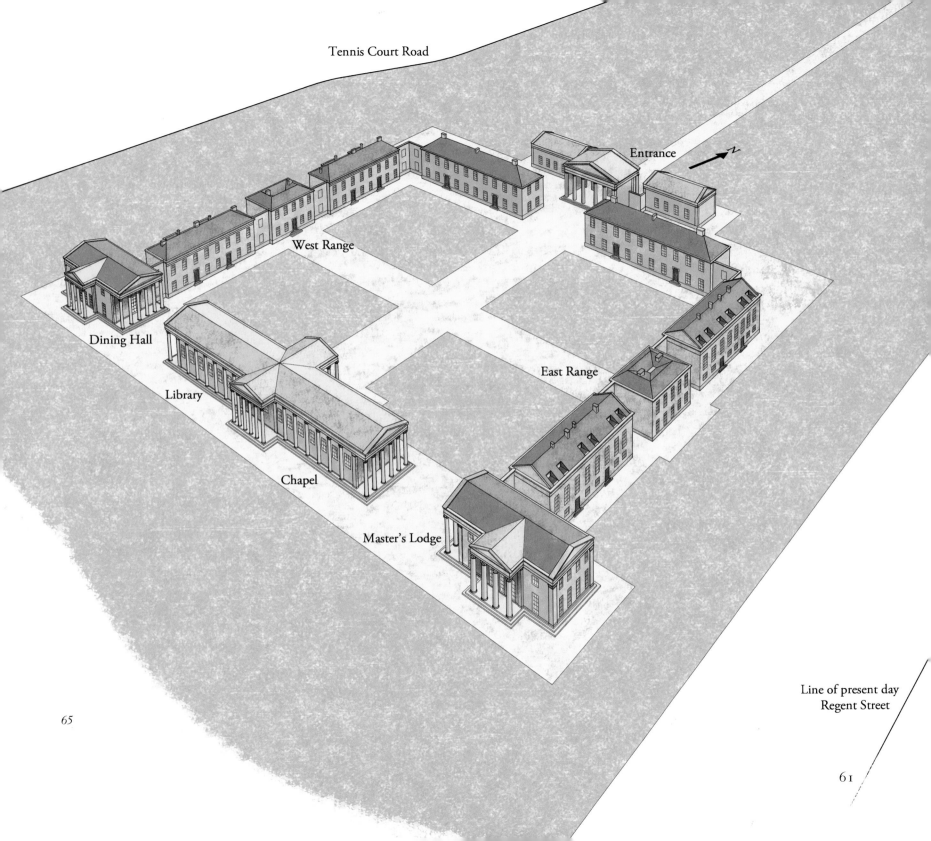

Tennis Court Road

Entrance

West Range

Dining Hall

Library

Chapel

East Range

Master's Lodge

Line of present day
Regent Street

65

61

leading into the court through a grand Propylaeum or gateway flanked by a porters' lodge and lecture room (figs. 65 and 67), the portico being modelled on the Propylaea in Athens. Various adaptations were made on this plan over the coming years, such as one scheme in 1817–18, in which the entrance composition was moved to the north end of the avenue (fig. 66), where it created a grander statement from Downing Street, as opposed to some simple iron gates that were later placed there.

In laying out his composition, Wilkins played a number of clever games with both plan and elevation. By breaking away from traditional continuous ranges enclosing a court, to form a more open "campus" plan, defined by buildings as separated blocks linked only by screen walls, attention was focused on the individual façades looking into the enclosure as elevations in their own right. The breaks between the buildings, created by the screen walls and to the south by the open corners, accentuated the lateral compositions and strengthened the all-important diagonal views across the open space from the corners. This was particularly true of the flanking porticos to the south-west and south-east created by the gaps at either end of the Library/Chapel range facing the Master's Lodge to the east and the Hall to the west. The component parts created a dominant north–south axis maximising the architectural effect: the entrance Propylaeum to the north and the main range of the Library/Chapel to the south connected strongly with each other as the monumental *tours de force* of the composition (figs. 68 and 69). The South Range in particular was the showpiece of Wilkins' design (figs. 74 and 75). Set like a Greek temple upon the triple-stepped *crepidoma* base, it was linked by this platform to the two terminating pavilions of the East and West Ranges. Although forming a continuous link at ground level it allowed space above to flow in and out of the campus composition as a whole, rather than being a self-contained unit separated from it.

Wilkins also played games with the classical orders and in the way he placed columns within porticos, often breaking with expected symmetry and rhythms, flouting the rules of classical composition. The transition of orders is satisfying, beginning with the approach to the entrance Propylaeum down the avenue from the north with sturdy and masculine Greek Doric columns without bases (fig. 67), as befitted an entrance composition; changing in the court to the feminine and elegant Ionic that surrounds all the main buildings in the south (fig. 74), more appropriate for the Library, Chapel, Hall and Master's Lodge. Within the Chapel itself, Wilkins had planned to introduce the decorative Corinthian order (fig. 76). On entering the court through the portico of the Propylaeum one would be

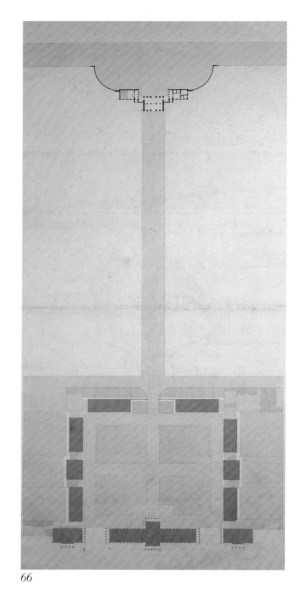

66

66. *Revised plan of the College, 1817–18, showing the entrance composition in the north to Downing Street. Downing College Archive.*

67. *The intended entrance to the College, etching by R. B. Harraden from the original by William Wilkins. RIBA Library Drawings and Archives Collections.*

Drawn by R.B.Harraden Jun.r from the Original by W.Wilkins Esq.r   Etched by Elizabeth Byrne.

Entrance to

DOWNING COLLEGE.

Published Jan.y 20.th 1809, by R.Harraden & Son Cambridge & by R.Cribb & Son, 288,Holborn,London.

67

68. View from the north, showing the entrance to the College.

69. View from the south, showing the unbuilt Chapel and Library range in the centre foreground, and the unbuilt north range and entrance in the distance.
Model made by Andrew Ingham Associates, London, for The Age of Wilkins exhibition at the Fitzwilliam Museum, Cambridge, 2000. Downing College Collection.

70. View from the east.

71. View from the west.

72. *The entrance Propylaeum.*

Views of the model to give an idea of the environment of the College if it had been fully completed.

75. *The extensive South Range, with Hall to the left (west), Library and Chapel as the central block, and Master's Lodge to the right (east).*

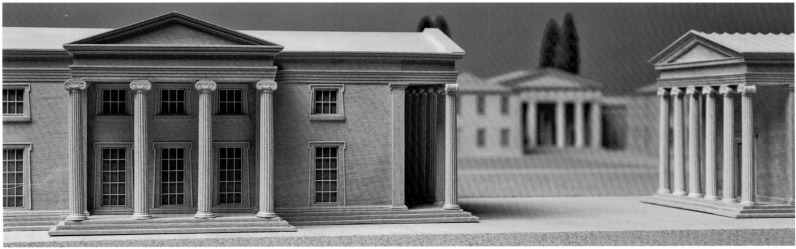

73. *View from the Hall and west end of the Library towards the main College entrance.*

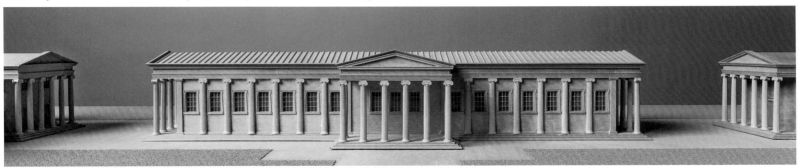

74. *View of the Chapel and Library from within the quadrangle, flanked by the Master's Lodge to the left (east), and the Hall to the right (west).*

confronted by the remarkable composition of buildings with repeating porticos and columns overwhelmingly greeting the eye. There was a playful and unconventional break in rhythm here: the outer main north portico of the entrance Propylaeum was composed of six columns, whereas the inner side was only of four; furthermore, the inner main portico of the south Library/Chapel range facing the north entrance did not mirror the four columns of the inner portico of the Propylaeum, but instead repeated the outer with six. In Wilkins' original design, later changed for the three architect judges, the four-column portico of the inner Propylaeum was repeated on the east and west ends of the South Range facing the inner porticos of both the Master's Lodge and the Hall, which had facing compositions to match. These were all later changed to six columns, but four-column compositions were used on the southern porticos of the Master's Lodge and Hall, thus repeating the south-facing Propylaeum on the outer court sides. Thus, all six-columned porticos in the College faced north, east and west; all four-columned porticos faced south, with the one exception being that of the Library/Chapel range, the stature of which justified the primary grandeur of six (fig. 75).

The public buildings on the main north–south axis were the dominant feature of Wilkins' composition, whereas the purely residential East and West Ranges were plain in their elevations, known as "astylar" in classical architecture, meaning without columns or pilasters. Stark though they were in character, their overall proportion and in particular the tapering treatment of the window and door openings, created a subtle elegance that is in itself very attractive, especially with the variety of yellow, orange and pink hues of the Ketton stone which can give a striking effect in certain lights (see fig. 4, pp. 10–11). On the whole, Wilkins was very sparing in his use of decoration even in the main public buildings, either owing to budgetary constraint or to his deliberately austere approach, and though only little is to be found in entablature mouldings, column and capital heads, it is of the highest quality (figs. 78-79). A delightful recurring feature is that of lions' heads used externally as gargoyles (fig. 80), and internally as a repeating motif around the entablature of the Hall (fig. 81).

When building began on 27 November 1806, it was decided to give priority to the provision of accommodation by building the East Range first to complete the Master's Lodge, the Professor of Medicine's house for Sir Busick Harwood (now the East Lodge), and the range in between for the temporary residences of Professor Christian and the Fellows John Lens, William Meek and William Frere. During

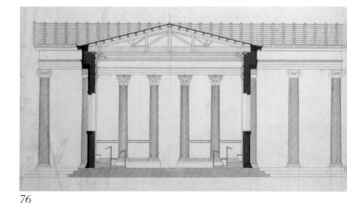

76

77

76. Drawing of Wilkins' unbuilt Chapel showing the use of the Corinthian order. Downing College Archive.
77. Typical staircase entrance in the West Range, showing the elegant tapering door and window openings.
78–81. The high-quality detailing of Wilkins original buildings in the College.

78

79

80

81

that winter, all the groundwork was undertaken, including the foundations, and the foundation stone was laid on 18 May 1807, a date celebrated annually to this day by a formal Commemoration of the College's benefactors, with a service in the Chapel followed by a dinner in the Hall, as a high point of the College year. The Master's Lodge was completed by the end of the year, by which time Wilkins found himself in conflict with both the Master and Professor Harwood, who effectively began to behave as though they were private clients with regard to the building of what they deemed to be their own houses, both demanding changes and alterations. This was also the case later with Professor Christian and the design of his house in the middle of the West Range (now the West Lodge), all parties being unhappy with Wilkins' inadequate handling of the plans, reflecting the inexperience of the young architect in this area of domestic layout. The Master, Francis Annesley, was particularly difficult and autocratic in his approach, demanding more and more space for his garden and even outbuildings for his own use. Annesley died in 1812 to be succeeded by the second Master, William Frere (1812–36), who grated with the architect even more by erecting sheds for his cows, pigs and sheep, allowing them to graze freely around the Lodge and on the lawns of the main court (fig. 82). Things soon came to a head owing to the already limited building fund. Construction ground to a halt at the Professor of Medicine's house midway along the East Range, at which point the Fellowship reviewed the situation, drastically reducing the building schedule and cutting back on what could be built. In his frustration, Wilkins proposed a scheme to the College to capitalise on its one major asset: the huge amount of land that it possessed on this spacious site just off the centre of Cambridge. He put forward an ingenious plan creating an extensive housing development, mainly in the northern area of the site but also along the boundary to the west of the main court, along what is now Tennis Court Road (fig. 83). He made a slight adjustment to the plan of the main quadrangle by moving the entrance composition further to the north, separating it from the North Range and making it a composition in its own right, flanked by two detached houses on either side. Facing this to the north were two rows of terraced houses to east and west, set at right angles to the approach avenue from Downing Street, which itself was to be lined by long rows of terraces, thirty houses on each side. In all, this great idea offered over one hundred properties to the College for leasehold sale or rental, ostensibly a most fitting solution to Downing's financial problems; but, alas, nothing came of it. Such an idea would not only have provided considerable revenue to the poor embryonic College, but would also have created a most appropriate use of the site in this area, introducing housing in a park environment comparable to other renowned English towns of similar

82

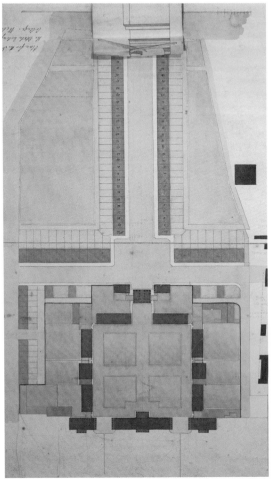

83

82. *The Master's Lodge, as the first completed building of the College, published for R. Ackermann's History of Cambridge 1814. Downing College Archive.*

83. *Plan by William Wilkins for the improvement of the College estate by the addition of a housing scheme of over one hundred units, 1817. Downing College Archive.*

character, such as Bath, Tunbridge Wells or Oxford. The College sold off this northern area of the Pembroke Leys to the University some eighty years later, resulting in the claustrophobic brick, concrete and tarmac jungle that is the "Downing Site" today. Doing so raised funds for necessary building works at the time, but in the long term the land sale was neither advantageous financially, nor desirable environmentally for a future northern neighbour to the College (see fig. 207, p. 194).

Wilkins continued to petition Frere and by 1818 enough money was borrowed to begin work on the West Range, though the north end of the East Range remained incomplete. Though he had built the Master's Lodge as the south termination of the East Range – west- and south-facing Ionic porticos giving some grandeur to the buildings and hinting at the Greek style – Wilkins had not yet had a chance to excel and show the potential of his concept. Now at last the Hall, as the matching termination of the West Range, would allow him to do so. Although he did not know it at the time, this was to be the only monumental interior that would be completed in the College and "through the serene proportions and colour scheme, the architect successfully recaptured an antique classical interior. The hall was surrounded by *giallo antico* [ornamental marble] pilasters of scagliola . . . alternating with Greek tapered openings and panels."[13] Wilkins' choice of the scagliola material to imitate a marble finish on the columns and pilasters (see figs. 178-185) was very much of the moment, as the firm of Croggon had only begun to produce it in 1818,[14] showing that the architect had his finger firmly on the pulse of contemporary trends in architectural manufacturing of the period. However, for most of the College's life the Hall interior was not as it is today, since the building was internally divided with the Hall occupying two-thirds of the space to the east, with the other third to the west being the Senior Combination Room, as shown in the plan detail of 1806 (fig. 84) and the aquatint from the same period (fig. 85). Across the whole width of the east end there was a full-height screen wall creating a narrow passage, which contained a staircase to a gallery with three small windows into the east portico. The main entrance was from a door in the east portico, via the narrow passageway from which two inner doors gave access to the Hall itself. At the west end, above the Senior Combination Room, there was an "Upper Room" that was used as a chapel, serving the College for over a century until the current chapel was built in the North Range in 1950 to 1953. It was not until the late 1960s that the Hall eventually took its current form of one large space, when a new detached Senior Combination Room was built to the immediate west (see fig. 99). With the removal of the old Senior Combination Room and the old chapel room

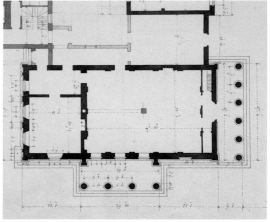

84

84. Plan detail of the Hall in its original form when subdivided at the west end to accommodate the Senior Combination Room with a Chapel room above. Also showing the two screen entrance doors from the east through a narrow corridor from the main entrance in the east portico. Downing College Archive.

85. Aquatint of the Hall viewed from the west end looking east, showing the two entrance doors from the screen corridor. Downing College Collection.

85

above, the Hall was able to occupy the entire building. Based on a double square, this resulted in the outstanding interior of today (see chapter 6, p. 163).

The West Range was completed in May 1821, giving the fledgling College adequate accommodation and facilities to house its members and admit its first undergraduates. Poor Wilkins must by now have begun to accept that his College would probably never be completed in full (fig. 86), and for many years until his death in 1839 he lived close by in a classical-style house in Lensfield Road opposite the southern boundary of the site, endlessly pondering the fate of his first major commission, which, had it been fully realised, would have undoubtedly been his masterpiece. Though incomplete, the Downing commission did bring Wilkins to prominence, and he was to gain many other commissions in the years to follow, including major buildings for other Cambridge colleges, such as King's, Trinity and Corpus Christi, all in neo-Gothic, as well as national commissions among them University College and the National Gallery in London, again in the classical style.

Nothing more happened architecturally in Downing until 1834 when a small house was built on the east side towards Regent Street to accommodate a member of staff who would also attend to this side-entrance gate, in later years to become the main entrance of the College and the Porters' Lodge of today (fig. 87). This new side access with gates and, effectively, a building constituting a porter's lodge, must have caused Wilkins concern in that it threatened to compromise the main north–south axis of his composition, creating a competing east–west cross–axis as a potential nail in the coffin of his intended layout for the College.

Only long after Wilkins' death was any further progress made with the buildings, when more funding became available in 1873 and the College appointed an architect to complete the East and West Ranges. Edward Middleton Barry (1830–1880) was one of five sons of the more famous father, Sir Charles Barry (1795–1860), architect of the Houses of Parliament along with A. W. N. Pugin. Edward was to complete that project after his father's death in 1860, as well as design the Royal Opera House in Covent Garden in 1857–8. The completion of the ranges at Downing between 1874 and 1876 was thus a small project, but Barry did not seek to exert his own ideas and followed faithfully the design precedent set by Wilkins. As Sicca states, Barry's contribution to the completion of the main ranges at Downing has hitherto been underestimated, and his achievement in this fundamentally important task of terminating both ranges to the north was superb.[15] Here, Barry totally respected

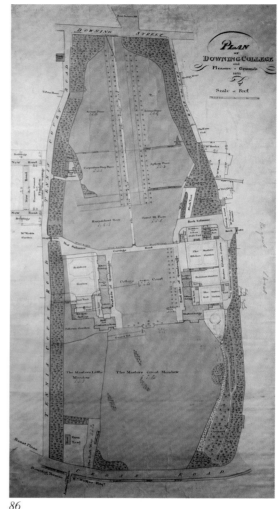

86

86. William Wilkins' plan of the College, 1822, showing the state of building progress on the east and west ranges, at which point construction of his buildings ceased, and the architect's desired tree planting scheme around the perimeter of the site. Downing College Archive.

87. The Porters' Lodge to Regent Street.

87

Wilkins and drew inspiration from the conceiving architect's design of the west elevation of the Hall (fig. 100): he treated his two "gable" elevations as pseudo-porticos with paired Ionic pilasters reflecting those of Wilkins and supporting full triangular pediments to top it all off convincingly (figs. 88 and 89). Furthermore, he also carried through Wilkins' beautifully tapered window openings at both floor levels, creating an elegant composition to complete the only two components of Wilkins' masterful concept. In response to the decision to establish the main entrance to the College from Regent Street in the east, Barry appropriately faced his northern terminations of both ranges in Ketton stone. In the original scheme, where the main entrance and route through the College was from north to south, these unimportant east and west façades were to be finished in the local yellow-grey gault brick (fig. 90).

Edward Barry was indeed a talented and versatile architect, a sensitive artist in the mould of Wilkins. His other work in the College mainly involved improvements to internal planning in both the East and West Lodges, but his most striking internal creation was to provide a focal point in the Hall by re-modelling the east end with paired Ionic columns, between which there is now a recently installed monumental sash-window supporting an elaboration of the Downing family arms, encompassing the College shield, the whole composition superbly framing the Master's Lodge through the window in the distance, as if a Greek temple set on the open plain (see fig. 91).

The extent of Wilkins' Downing College was thus as complete as it would ever be, along with the exceptional finishing touches applied by Edward Barry. With only the two flanking residential ranges finished and the two key components un-built – the Propylaeum and the South Range of the Library and Chapel – it is hard to imagine what the effect of Wilkins' completed scheme would have been. The orientation of the site today is on the dominant east–west axis where one enters across the site from a side entrance in the east, rather than from north to south as Wilkins intended. He also planned his site to be surrounded by a dense planting of trees (see fig. 64 and 86), separating the College from the town, with the central domus as an open space of expansive lawns with beautiful buildings rising out of an Arcadian plain broken only with the occasional tall and slender cypress. Over the last few decades the visual impact of the architecture within the quadrangle has been severely compromised by the planting of too many trees. In 1990, Anthony Talbot Williams, then President of the Downing Association, expressed his concern in the annual newsletter: "But amongst all the improvements has the tree planting been overdone? The spacious court is

88

89

90

88 and 89. E. M. Barry's completion of the northern terminations of the East and West Ranges.

90. The original brick facade of the West Range.

91. Barry's east end paired Ionic columns in the Hall.

91

Downing's unique architectural heritage. Not for us the claustrophobia of other colleges. But the trees now obscure most of the chapel end of the court and before long will hide it completely. Trees are magnificent in their place: the Master's Lodge Garden, the Fellows Garden, and behind the buildings, giving a beautiful backdrop; but I hope the young forest in the court will not be allowed to go unculled."[16] Alas, his prophetic words now ring true, and the College, now fully aware of the problem, has recently commissioned a master plan by the landscape architect, Alice Foxley of Studio Karst. It can only be hoped that, in the future, the site of Downing may be restored to what it was always intended to be.

Notes
1 Watkin: *Architect King*, p. 125.
2 Willis and Clark, 1886, vol. II, p. 756.
3 Sicca, p. 22.
4 Willis and Clark, 1886, vol. II, pp. 756–7.
5 Bicknell, pp. 4–5.
6 Hope, p. 33.
7 Colvin, p. 177.
8 Sicca, p. 131.
9 Ibid., p. 40.
10 Ibid., p. 48.
11 Ibid.
12 Downing College Muniments, DCAR/1/2/2/6/2/1.
13 Sicca, p. 73.
14 Ibid.
15 Ibid., p. 79.
16 "President's Foreword", *Downing College Association Newsletter* 1990, p. 4.

92. *View of the Master's Lodge from the North Range.*

93 *(overleaf) The Master's Lodge from the Master's Garden.*

92

94. The Master's Lodge from the north-west.

95. The Master's Lodge from the south-east.   96 (overleaf). Detail of the Ionic portico of the Master's Lodge from the quadrangle.

97. The Drawing-room, the Master's Lodge.

98. The Dining-room, the Master's Lodge. 99 (overleaf) The Hall and Senior Combination Room from the Fellows' Garden.

100. The Hall from the south-west.

101. The Hall from the east.

102. The Hall porticos from the south-east.   103. A typical Wilkins staircase in the West Range.

4 Twentieth-century architects to 1983

Downing's poor financial state continued throughout the Victorian period, the erosion of much of the endowment funds having an enduring and damaging effect on the future development of the College, profoundly compromising its growth and thwarting the plans of any architect who became involved. With no significant funds to draw on, the College inevitably turned to its one major asset, its wonderfully spacious site on the edge of town of which the College itself had so far only occupied about one quarter (see fig. 86). However, instead of adopting Wilkins' clever idea of 1817 to develop the site with the addition of housing for long-term and ongoing financial benefit, the Governing Body sold off the whole northern area piecemeal to the University between 1895 and 1907. This was a time when the University was undergoing massive change and needed to expand, especially in the sciences where central city space was required for the building of new departments and laboratories. The vacant tract of land at the north end of the huge site was ideal for such expansion at that time, with its close proximity to many of the colleges. Perhaps it was this collective need within the Cambridge academic community in this period that partly swayed the Downing Fellowship into agreeing to the sale of some of their land. Beneficial though it may have been at a time of great financial need, it would do little to help the College's financial future in the long term. At this time, the College also decided to develop the southern perimeter of the site, and from 1895 the red-brick villas along the northern edge of Lensfield Road (fig. 105) were built and let on 99-year leases, most of which have gradually reverted to the College and are now student accommodation backing onto the Paddock with direct access to the domus.

In the early years of the new century undergraduate numbers were on the increase. In Downing not only was more accommodation becoming a pressing need, but the lack of both a proper chapel and library had still to be addressed. In 1910 student unrest in the College came to a head when a petition was submitted to the Governing Body complaining about cramped conditions, along with the sum of £70 10s, the first proceeds of an undergraduate fund-raising campaign primarily for provision of a chapel and increased accommodation. Since the beginning, worship in Downing had taken place in the poky makeshift Chapel above the Senior Combination Room (fig. 106), at the west end of the Hall.

105

106

104. *The Senior Combination Room.*

105. *The Lensfield Road villas as the southern boundary to the College site.*

106. *The Chapel room formerly above the Hall, which served the College for more than a century until the current chapel was built in the early 1950s.*

An interesting suggestion put forward at that time for an affordable, proper place of worship, was to build an iron-structured chapel taking advantage of the technological advances that had taken place in the use of cast iron as an exciting new building material. To many in the Fellowship this idea was abhorrent, for such structures were associated with industrial buildings arising from the Industrial Revolution, epitomised by Joseph Paxton's pre-fabricated iron and glass Crystal Palace built in London half a century earlier for the Great Exhibition of 1851. Although building an iron church must have seemed very odd to many traditional Edwardians, this trend had already become fashionable in France with several leading Parisian architects building churches there using iron between 1854 and 1904.[1] Inevitably, the proposal at Downing failed, but this brief dalliance with such an advanced engineering idea of the time was to foreshadow a successful infiltration of the domus with a similar modernist approach some sixty years later.

Bowing to the continuing demands of the student body for further accommodation, the College in 1914 commissioned the architect, C. G. Hare to provide designs for a new building containing twenty sets of rooms and a chapel and library. This was to be located in the north-west corner of the now reduced site, in the area that is today occupied by Kenny Court. What Hare put forward was a fairly monumental building (fig. 107), clearly too large to be tucked away in the north-west corner, and one which was more than likely intended as a northern termination to Wilkins' quadrangle as defined by his East and West Ranges. Hare's approach totally ignored the Wilkins precedent, however, and stylistically was out of keeping with the pure Grecian style of the original buildings. Nevertheless, his large mansion-like "pile" in an Edwardian Classicism, more reminiscent of the English Baroque of Wren, Vanbrugh and Hawksmoor from the early eighteenth century, found such favour with the Fellowship that Downing's first-ever public appeal was launched to raise the funding. The First World War then intervened, and fortunately Hare's scheme was never to see the light of day. No further building progress was to take place for another fifteen years, but in the meantime, in order to ease the ongoing desperate lack of accommodation, in the mid-1920s the two Professors' houses in the East and West Ranges were converted for general use.

It was not until 1929 that the next major stage in the development of Downing's buildings began when the College engaged the eminent colonial architect, Sir Herbert Baker (1862–1946), to give his opinion on how the site should be developed and what approach the College should take in the future. Baker was one of the leading

107. The proposed new building of 1914 by C. G. Hare. Downing College Collection.

New Buildings DOWNING COLLEGE Cambridge

107

British architects of his generation, working on large-scale projects in South Africa for Cecil Rhodes; in India alongside Edwin Lutyens on Government buildings in New Delhi; and later, back in England, on such buildings as his War Memorial Cloister at Winchester College, Hampshire (1924), India and South Africa Houses in London (1930 and 1933), and his enlargement of Sir John Soane's Bank of England (1925–39). The College held Baker in such high regard that he was made an Honorary Fellow in 1932, and a long and fruitful relationship developed until his death in 1946, continuing for some time after with his partner Alex Scott.

Baker's initial brief was to provide designs for new buildings in the north-east corner of the site between Regent Street and Wilkins' East Range, a distinct change of policy from building in the opposite north-west corner as had been the intention before the First World War. The idea now was to develop the entrance vicinity between the Porters' Lodge and the quadrangle. However, once in the hands of the architect, this soon expanded into the whole northern area fully spanning the site from east to west. The central component of his proposal was a clever and generous play on Wilkins' original South Range, putting back a Library and Chapel into the court composition, as well as a Common Room, flanked on either side by extensive accommodation blocks (figs. 108 and 109). The central Entrance Hall between Library and Chapel was also to be topped by an elegant saucer dome accentuating Wilkins' primary north–south axis down the middle of the court. That new, key building was to be roughly in the position of the originally intended Propylaeum, possibly in further homage to Wilkins. However, given that the former north–south axis of Wilkins' original design concept had by now been lost for ever through the sale of the northern site area, Baker concentrated on turning the axis through ninety degrees to create a strong, new and dominant entrance axis running east to west, out of what had become a compromised side-entrance solution. This was to be the new focal vista stretching across the site from Regent Street to Tennis Court Road, establishing a new cross-spinal strength to the overall composition, albeit a complete change of orientation from what the original architect had intended. The superb effect of this idea can be seen in the perspective water-colour of 1929 by H. G. Pilkington from the new front gate (figs. 110 and 111), showing the sequence of porticos running across the site with a triumphal arch terminating the composition to Tennis Court Road in the distance. While this admirable scheme worked perfectly in plan, the architecture was not Greek in style but Roman classical in origin, though acceptable enough in its convincing play on, and adaptation of, Wilkins' original design.

108 and 109. Sir Herbert Baker's vision for Downing of 1929–30, showing his concept to terminate Wilkins' quadrangle to the north. Downing College Archive.

109

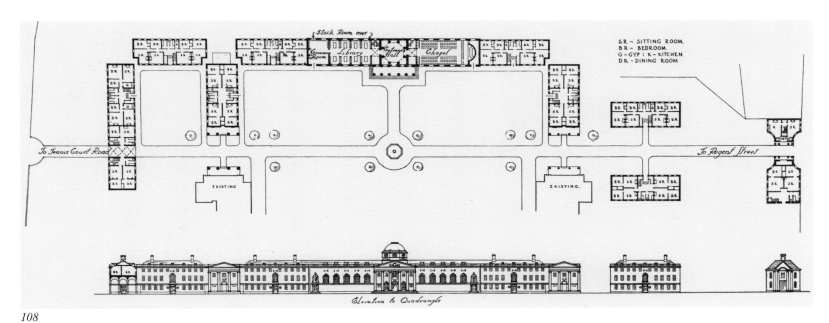

108

110

110. Sir Herbert Baker's Entrance and Porters' Lodge to Regent Street, 1929–30. Downing College Archive.

111. H. G. Pilkington's perspective view of Sir Herbert Baker's scheme, showing the new east-west axis across the site from Regent Street in the east to Tennis Court Road in the west, 1929. Downing College Archive.

11

A. L. C. Pilkington
1939

In detail, Baker also echoed Wilkins with his three new porticos: six-columned on the central Entrance Hall between the Chapel and Library, akin to the main porticos of both the Master's Lodge and Hall; and four-columned on the terminations of the east and west wings, replicating the south porticos of the older buildings. He also proposed to apply matching four-columned porticos on the Barry-completed northern terminations of both the East and West Ranges, to mirror those on his facing wings, though they were never executed.

In 1930 the College launched an appeal to raise funds for Baker's proposal, producing an elaborate brochure with illustrations by the architect. But Baker's scheme, like Wilkins' before him, was not to be built in full, and only the two east and west corner wings were to be completed between 1930 and 1932. Building progress once again came to a halt through lack of funds, only to be reviewed briefly in 1939 when the new Master, Admiral Sir Herbert Richmond, suggested making economies to the Baker scheme. With the outbreak of the Second World War all further building stopped, and the College was occupied throughout the war years by the RAF. Baker died in February 1946, and in September of that year Richmond made his own adaptations to Baker's plans shown in a sketch, which he circulated in a memorandum to the Fellowship stating that: "The Entrance Hall and Combination Room, handsome and dignified though they be, serve no practical purpose, and may even be considered to some degree as pretentious. The Dome, in my eyes, is a costly excrescence besides being out of harmony with the restrained simplicity of the original buildings. Neither Entrance Hall, Combination Room nor Dome are revenue producing."[2] As his competent sketch proposal illustrates (fig. 113), Richmond was severely pragmatic in his thinking; he wanted to simplify the central block by doing away with the Library and Combination Room, but retaining a chapel placed transversely across the range north-to-south flanked by even more accommodation. Furthermore, he suggested that the Master's Lodge should be converted into the College library, and the smaller West Lodge on the other side of the court used for the Master's accommodation. The majority of the Fellowship went along with Richmond, though not with the conversion of the Lodge into a library. Alex Scott (1887–1962), Baker's partner and successor in the firm, was asked to submit modifications to the original design, concentrating on the provision of a chapel and the additional accommodation.

Sir Herbert Richmond died in 1947, and between 1947 and 1949 Scott redesigned the centrepiece of the North Range between the two Baker wings (fig. 116), and also converted the East Lodge into a library. The new Chapel and accommodation were

112

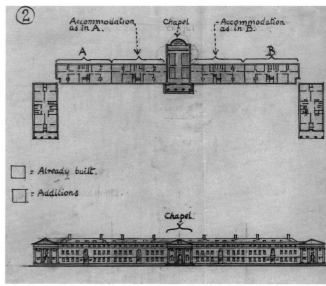

113

112. Baker's portico terminating the north-east angle building of the North Range, with the Chapel beyond.

113. Sir Herbert Richmond's sketch showing his alternative idea for Baker's centre section of the North Range. Downing College Archive.

114. Baker's north-west portico.

114

built between 1950 and 1953, with the Chapel along the lines of Richmond's transverse plan taking on Baker's six-columned portico of the former Entrance Hall as its southern entrance façade from the quadrangle, but omitting the saucer dome from the composition. The whole of the central block is named Graystone Building, after a bequest made by Sidney William Graystone (1862–1924), Fellow Commoner of the College.[3] The total capacity today of the Baker and Scott North Range buildings is 130 refurbished student rooms with accompanying kitchens. At last, the College now had a chapel (figs 117-29), albeit on an unconventional north–south axis, as opposed to the traditional east–west, and far less grand than intended by either Wilkins or Baker. The Chapel takes the simple form of a panelled ante-chapel upon entrance (fig. 119), leading to a short nave terminated by a pleasing apse at the north end, containing the altar, all "more reminiscent of a Romanesque church than of a Greek temple".[4]

The end of the long Baker/Scott era came in the early 1960s when Alex Scott and Vernon Helbing, another partner in the firm, again modified the original scheme to the west, reducing the intended larger side-court flanking Tennis Court Road to two individual blocks built in 1960 to 1961. These buildings were funded by Agnes and Muriel Kenny, daughters of a former Downing Professor of Law, Courtney Stanhope Kenny (1847–1930), and were named Kenny Court (fig. 130), today providing fifty-one refurbished student rooms. A recent refurbishment of the entire access and car-parking area along the northern side of the College, funded by the Howard Foundation, has ensured that the Kenny buildings and the entire North Range are finally backed by high-quality surfaces suitable for vehicle and covered bicycle parking, along with plantings, railings, and even an electric-car charging point.

Baker's involvement at Downing was severely criticised by the great architectural scholar, Sir Nikolaus Pevsner, when he stated: "Downing called for nothing but a faithful completion of as much as possible of Wilkins' plan . . . the architect abandoned Wilkins's design just enough to irritate. The L-shaped ranges which he added to the north-west and north-east in 1930-31 . . . are inferior in every way to Wilkins's". That Baker had to accommodate three instead of two storeys was to satisfy a college demand, but the fussy oval windows, the doorcases, the quoins and the balustrades seem hardly justifiable."[5] Pevsner clearly did not like Baker's choice of Roman classical in place of Wilkins' pure Greek; his squeezing of three storeys into buildings of the same two-storey height as the Wilkins originals; or the deviation from Wilkins' austere elegance towards fanciful and unnecessary touches of flamboyance. Sicca admirably takes up the defence of Baker on this fundamental

115

115. As with Wilkins, a fine and bold Ionic order in the Baker buildings.

116. View of the North Range and Chapel, with Graystone Building as the central block, by Alex Scott, from the north-east portico.

117 (overleaf). The Chapel from the south.

116

118. *Chapel interior looking south.* 119. *The nave and apse from the ante-chapel in the south.*

118

QUÆRERE · VERUM

121

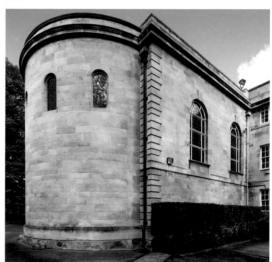

122

120 (left). College arms on the ante-chapel screen.

121. Brass ram's head door-handle to the Chapel.

122. The Chapel to the north.

123. Advent carol service, 2014.

124–128 (overleaf). Stained-glass around the Chapel apse by L. C. Evetts (1962–63), showing the four horsemen of the Apocalypse.

124

125

126

127

128

129. *The new Chapel organ.*

130

130. Kenny Court.

131. A typical Baker staircase in the North Range.

131

question of how any contemporary architect can achieve a faithful completion of, or additions to, buildings of such defining historical style, concluding that this problem "constitutes the core of the college's architectural dilemma in the latter part of the twentieth century [Sicca was writing in 1987]". She went on to ask: "Should a replica of an early nineteenth-century building be erected in the twentieth century? Or should the college maintain faith in Wilkins' vision, but find contemporary classicist expression of that vision?"[6] Downing has continued pursuing the latter, healthier approach, which has resulted in an exciting mixture of modern additions to the domus, ranging from one classical extreme to the other, both inevitably courting controversy.

Now that the College possessed a proper chapel, attention was directed to returning the Hall into the state that Wilkins might well have intended, by taking out the Senior Combination Room (SCR) at the west end and the old chapel room above, and at last transforming the interior into the beautifully elegant double-square space that we see today (for the current Hall, see pp 162–71, which deals with the most recent restoration). A new SCR was to be built separate to the Hall, along with an improved and enlarged two-storey kitchen and administrative block to the immediate north-west. A large number of architects were considered for this multifarious project,[7] ranging from traditionalists such as Raymond Erith, through to ultra-modernists of the time including Sir Denys Lasdun and James Stirling, both of whom were quickly deemed too extremist in their "modern movement" approaches. The practice chosen was the local firm of Howell, Killick, Partridge & Amis (HKPA), who were invited to submit their proposals in 1964. The head of the practice, Bill Howell (1922–1974) – later to become Cambridge Professor of Architecture in 1973 – consulted the eminent architectural historian and renowned classicist, Sir John Summerson (1904–1992), on the approach to the restoration of the Hall. Summerson recommended that the architects should work with the firm of Colefax and Fowler, who were the consultants for the interior.[8] The colour scheme at this time was based on two colours: an orange for the walls, inspired by the orange/brown colour of the mock-marbling or scagliola technique used by both Wilkins and later Barry for the pilasters and columns; and a lighter stone colour that was used for the architectural elements, all of which can be seen in an old photograph (see fig.179, p. 164). The end result of this restoration was an admirable Georgian interior, the only one of its kind in either Oxford or Cambridge (see figs. on pp. 162–71), and very different to the traditional halls of other colleges that were largely modelled on those of medieval manor houses.

132. The Senior Combination Room and Hall from the Fellows' Garden.

The new Senior Combination Room was to be built close-by to the west and in line with the Hall, with the kitchen and administration block running behind both to the north, the SCR being the main external component of the overall scheme in a prominent position also facing the Fellows' Garden. The first design put forward by HKPA (fig. 133), was in a Le-Corbusier-style brutalism, a fashion typical of the mid-1960s. Although this did not go down well with most of the Fellowship, had the Master of the day, the classical scholar W. K. C. Guthrie, had his way, this is what would have been built. Guthrie wished to introduce a defined modernist flavour to the College, stating that in his opinion this first scheme had "a solid, monumental quality about it – modern, yes, but it looks good, and manages to be entirely in keeping with its neighbours without any hint of mere imitation".[9] One can see Guthrie's point as very much a man of his time, but the scheme was rejected by the Fellowship and the architects were asked to think again.

The revised approach of Bill Howell to the SCR saw a radical change of direction, with an ingenious response intended to satisfy both the traditionalist and modernist camps of the time: he combined the use of modern building materials and construction techniques with the roots of classical architecture, creating a basic post-and-lintel structure along the Vitruvian lines of the primitive hut and the classical temple. This was now a refreshing and playfully intellectual design in response to the setting, with the Greek Revival Hall and the Master's Lodge in close proximity (fig. 135). In both of Howell's schemes he acknowledged Wilkins by accentuating the horizontal emphasis in his compositions: his use of the three-stepped *crepidoma* podium-style platform on which ancient temples were set on the top step or *stylobate*, as with the Hall and the Master's Lodge; and his employment of the long connecting stone wall between the Hall and the SCR, behind which the kitchens and administration block are effectively concealed, a device inspired by Wilkins' screen walls linking his original pavilions. Howell's structure can also be easily related to that of Wilkins' main component buildings: his pre-cast concrete and Portland stone aggregate posts as Wilkins' rather more beautiful Ionic columns and pilasters; and his similar concrete lintels supporting the lively roof structure echoing the pediments on both the Hall and the Lodge; though Howell's reference to the Baroque here, by separating each angled section of the roof like "broken" pediments, would not have pleased the purist Wilkins.

Howell now satisfied the brief brilliantly by creating a clearly modern building that fitted into its classical environment through the reinterpretation of the historical forms that surrounded it, thereby reflecting the *genius loci* of the site – the pervading spirit of

133. Sketch showing the initial proposal for the new SCR from Howell, Killick, Partridge & Amis. Downing College Archive.

134. The SCR from the south-east.

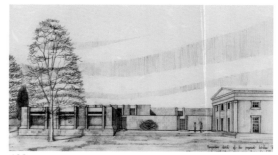

133

118

134

the place – admirably. In the design of the structure, devised in collaboration with the engineer, David Powell, the architect used paired columns to form both an outer and inner grid of posts, showing the structure both externally and internally, across which sit cantilevered beams that stretch into the middle of the room to support the main interior feature of the suspended central lantern, which weighs seven tons (fig. 104, p. 94). Again with reference to antique sources, the form of this central lantern is reminiscent of the *compluvium* opening in the atrium roof structure of a Greek or Roman house, its original function being to let in light as well as air. Reviews of this exciting little building have been very mixed, reflecting the impassioned responses such playing around with classical sources can ignite: "the combination room does prove . . . that reinterpretation can offer greater pleasure than reproduction", Walter Siegal, *Architects' Journal*, October 1969; "this travesty of a design . . . turns its back on the spirit of the original . . . go and see it in all its pristine ugliness", Marcus Binney, *Country Life*, August 1971; and "additions to Downing College are a model of intelligent grafting of new on to old and a demonstration that in doing so harmony of scale and materials are more important than similarity of style", J. M. Richards, *Times Literary Supplement*, August 1981. Writing in 2013, Otto Saumarez Smith refers to the SCR as "a gem of a building", and goes on to say: "The SCR is remarkable, both in its own time and in ours, for its unusual combination of the bristling confidence and audacity which is characteristic of much Sixties architecture, whilst simultaneously presenting an intelligent and witty dialogue with its classical neighbours."[10]

Notes
1 Sicca, pp. 81–2.
2 Ibid., p. 93.
3 The Graystone bequest was subject to a life interest which terminated in 1943 when the College received the funds.
4 Sicca, p. 95.
5 Pevsner, p. 68.
6 Sicca, p. 96.
7 Ibid.
8 *Downing College: The Redecoration of the Hall*, 12 July 1968, Downing College Archives, DCAR/1/2/8/1/63.
9 W. K. C. Guthrie, letter of 21 April 1966, Downing archives, DCAR/1/2/4/1/47.
10 Saumarez Smith, p. 149.

135. The Senior Combination Room in line with its Classical neighbours of the Hall and the Master's Lodge in the distance.

135

5 Contemporary Downing and the architecture of Quinlan and Francis Terry

"The College still needs a Library", declared Peter Bicknell, Fellow in Architecture at Downing, in 1982, stressing that since the outset it had been "housed in makeshift premises".[1] He also identified an urgent newer need "for a large general activities room for junior members such as most Cambridge colleges have been able to provide", and reminded his readers of the "need for more 'chambers' within the Domus". He expressed the hope that before long the funds would be forthcoming, but could not have expected his vision to become a reality so soon. Within a few years funds were indeed forthcoming, and a new era in Downing's architectural history dawned, made possible through the munificence of two Downing men: Dr Alan N. Howard (1929–), Honorary Fellow and inventor of the Cambridge Diet, through the charitable Howard Foundation, which he founded; and Mr Joseph Maitland Robinson (1905–1989), who had read History at Downing in the 1920s and was then involved in the wireless communications industry, where he later made his fortune in the early days of television rentals.[2] Over the next three decades the Howard Foundation was to provide the College with three new buildings forming Howard Court – the Howard Building, Howard Lodge and the Howard Theatre – and Mr Maitland Robinson was responsible for the new Library in his name. The College also built a new Junior Combination Room named the Butterfield Building, and Richmond House, a commercial block facing Regent Street. The buildings were designed initially by Quinlan Terry (1937–), then by Quinlan & Francis Terry Architects, when Quinlan's son, Francis (1969–), a Cambridge-trained architect and Downing graduate (1988–94), joined the practice.

The first gift from the Howard Foundation in 1984 meant the College had again to choose either a modern or classical architect, the first time since the new SCR scheme in 1964. The architectural climate of the 1980s was quite different to that of twenty years earlier: the brutal modernism inspired by the 1930s "Modern Movement" style had now given way to a variety of contemporary building styles, with the latest form of Post-Modern Classicism slowly becoming fashionable via North America and the Continent. While there was this wider choice, there was also more interference and control over clients by conservationist lobbies and the Royal Fine Arts Commission in one direction, and strict RIBA (Royal Institute of British Architects) competition

136. The Howard Theatre.

rules in another, with such competitions being dominated by judges still inevitably favouring modernist architects.[3] At the time, there was also the scandal over the competition for the extension to the National Gallery in London, where the American architect, Robert Venturi – also adding to a William Wilkins building – fell foul of public opinion; the mood expressed so forcibly in Prince Charles' resounding catch-phrase in his speech at the RIBA 150th anniversary dinner in 1984 when he famously labelled the proposed extension "a monstrous carbuncle on the face of a much loved and elegant friend". This scandal came about through an RIBA-elected panel disregarding the wishes of the gallery's trustees (the client) and forcing a design on the gallery that clashed controversially with its surroundings in Trafalgar Square. Downing College did not wish to embark on this process of open competitions in which it might also have little control and find itself forced to build something not to its liking. A more traditional approach was thus adopted whereby senior members of the College were asked to suggest architects for consideration from among whom they would make a choice without any formal competition taking place. A list of impressive international names was compiled, including Philip Johnson, Léon Krier, Sir Terry Farrell, Arata Isozaki, Arthur Erickson and Quinlan Terry.[4] Works by these architects were studied, some buildings visited, and Quinlan Terry was chosen by the College and the benefactor. In May 1983 the architect was then invited to submit designs for a new lecture theatre, a Junior Combination Room building, and a residential building, on the strength of which he was selected.

In 1987, Dr Cinzia Sicca, the architectural historian and driving force in the Fellowship for appointing Terry, said, "his buildings are so classical that they look as if designed by a seventeenth- or eighteenth-century architect. However, his originality lies in his profound understanding of the classical language of architecture, which enables him to expand and re-interpret it, sometimes in a whimsical fashion, while maintaining an absolute faithfulness to its principles and materials. Unlike other Post-Modern architects, whose classicism is mostly pastiche and often of a very ephemeral nature, Terry's buildings have the grace and long-lasting virtues of the monuments of past centuries."[5] In 2006, Professor David Watkin dubbed Terry "the single most distinguished and prolific architect at work in the classical tradition in either Britain or the United States of America". He went on to say that Terry "has attempted more completely than any other architect in Britain to pull the rug from beneath the false certainties of Modernism. At the same time, he is both modern and radical for, as he rightly claims, no one has the monopoly of the word 'Modern'."[6]

137

138

Terry had trained at the Architectural Association School of Architecture in London, during which time and after he had worked in the office of Stirling and Gowan before becoming a pupil of the traditionalist architect Raymond Erith in 1962, and a partner of Erith & Terry from 1966 until Erith's death in 1973.[7] Interestingly, Erith had been the runner-up at Downing for the SCR scheme in 1965, and some twenty years later Terry was to become the architect of the College. Francis Terry qualified as an architect in 1996, but then worked as a professional and very accomplished painter for several years before joining his father's practice. The firm operates from the picturesque village of Dedham in Essex, based in an old-fashioned, rambling high-street cottage, from where it designs buildings in England and Ireland, and around the world. The practice is based very much on the lines of traditional, artistic hand-drawing, and great pride is taken in developing all buildings from the drawing board to the building site. Only when Francis joined was computer-aided design introduced, but very much operating alongside their artistic approach to the craft of designing buildings. Both Quinlan and Francis Terry are very accomplished artists in the classical manner, as can be seen in the many drawings included here, and this quality is present in every building they create, from commercial developments such as Richmond Riverside (1984–7), through ecclesiastical as in Brentwood Cathedral, Essex (1989–91), the extraordinarily beautiful Regent's Park villas for the Crown Estate Commissioners (1989–2002), and the buildings at Downing (1985–2011).

Terry's first Downing commission, the Howard Building (1985–9, figs. 137-147) – the first Post-Modern Classical building in either Oxford or Cambridge – was to be tucked away in the West Lodge garden between the back of Wilkins' West Range and Tennis Court Road. This site was to be allocated for what would later be the new West Lodge Garden Quadrangle (fig. 149), now named Howard Court. The building provided the College with a long-awaited multi-functional auditorium on the upper floor, (figs. 141), and an elegant ground-floor reception room with a bar (fig. 144). The auditorium was originally built with an open trussed roof and no ceiling, the trusses sitting on a deep entablature supported by Ionic pilasters (fig. 143), but this was upgraded in 2014 with a new, coffered ceiling designed by Francis Terry, which has transformed the space into a more sophisticated interior (fig. 141), along with improved services throughout the building. Comfortably for the architect, this site was not in the vicinity of the determining Greek Revival architecture in the main court, as Howell's SCR had been some twenty years earlier, sitting next to the dominant Hall. In this location, the immediate neighbours were to

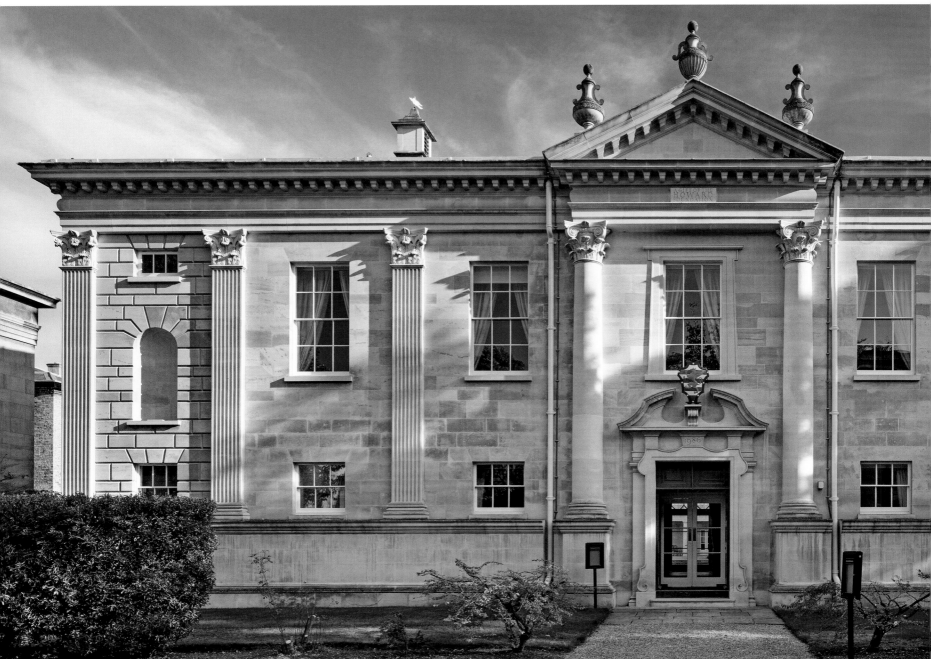

139 and 140. The main, north elevation of the Howard Building, and related drawing of the door by the architect. Drawing: courtesy of Quinlan and Francis Terry Architects.

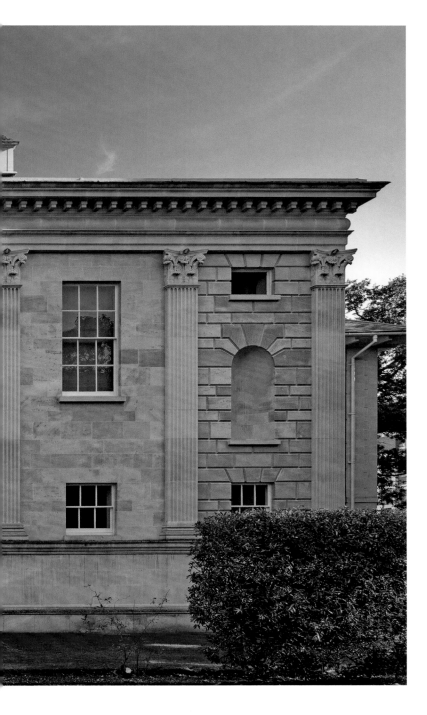

140

141. Howard Building auditorium, showing the new ceiling of 2014.

142. Composite column head, Howard Building.

143. Previous ceiling structure, Howard Building.

be Barry's stylish north end of the West Range (see fig. 89, p. 76); Scott's and Helbing's comparatively stark and plain Kenny Court (see fig. 130, p. 114); and Baker's lively north-west Ionic portico (see fig. 114, p. 103). Here, it was not to be Wilkins who dictated, instead the dialogue was to be with Barry and Sir Herbert Baker. The building is a blend of yellow to orange-brown Ketton stone for the walls, setting off the whiter Portland stone for the main structural members such as the plinth, pilasters, columns, entablature, door surrounds and the balustrade on the south side. The whole composition is playfully inventive – "I thought it would be fun to do something more Baroque"[8] – with a stronger connection to Baker's Roman classical than anything to do with Wilkins' Greek. The main, seven-bay elevation to the north (fig. 139) employs a giant order of pilasters, as in Barry's north façade, and the two engaged or semi-columns of the central section relate to Baker's portico, all sitting on a deep dado-style plinth. The order here, however, is not the Ionic of the auditorium, which dominates everywhere else in the College, but the more elaborate Corinthian topping the pilasters, and the flamboyant Composite on the columns, both more appropriate external features for a building of a theatrical nature. This mixture of elements and orders – pilasters and engaged columns, Corinthian and Composite – was inspired by Bramante's cloister of Santa Maria della Pace, Rome (1500–4), studied by Terry in 1967 when a Rome scholar.[9] The entrance bay, with its elaborate doorway topped by a broken pediment (figs 139 and 140), gives a particularly strong feeling of the Baroque, and above this urns decorate the small pediment to the roof. There is also a satisfying play in the surface treatment of the façade, from the smooth stonework of the five central bays transforming into rusticated end bays with niches, here absent of their intended urns (figs. 139). The rustication, plinth and Corinthian pilasters continue around both east (fig. 146) and west ends, to a southern façade that is comparatively plain in treatment. This has a projecting ground floor loggia or colonnade with columns in a mix of the Greek and Roman Doric orders (i.e. baseless but with capitals with Roman astragal detailing) supporting a pretty balustrade (fig. 145), inspired by the Piazza della Madonna at Loreto, studied and drawn by Terry in 1982.[10] By bringing in the Doric order here, Terry managed to incorporate all four of the ancient orders in one building, referred to by an admiring Dr Sicca as an architectural *tour de force*.

144. Ground-floor reception room and bar, Howard Building. 145. The Howard Building from the south-east, across the sunken garden.

Following pages: 146. East elevation of the Howard Building with Howard Lodge: 147. Howard Court, showing the Howard Theatre and Howard Lodge.

The next building to follow on this site was Howard Lodge (1994–5, fig. 147, previous pages), as the west range of what is now Howard Court, set at a slightly skewed angle to the Howard Building following the line of Tennis Court Road. It is a three-storeyed accommodation range in Ketton stone of eleven bays long, exhibiting an overall plain façade, but with the following features giving the building a very defined personality: the ground floor is set back behind the continuation of the Doric colonnade from the Howard Building, here operating as a covered walkway; a deep and rustic Tuscan cornice runs the whole length, through the central pediment, creating a strong feel of pastoral buildings from an Italian landscape; and a small Venetian window set in the projecting centre bay pleasingly breaks the repetitive pattern of the plain fenestration with a little hint of flamboyance. The building is very popular with students, providing thirty-two luxury en-suite rooms designed very much with the out-of-term conference market in mind.

The site of Howard Court, or the "West Lodge Garden Quadrangle", had for many years been a quiet, informal back garden of grass and trees, the only feature being the small but striking stone griffin that many older members of the College will remember, today relocated to the opposite side of the College in the East Lodge garden (fig. 148). The intended form of this new court was meant to stop at this point with the completion of Howard Lodge, the open south side to the kitchen service yard being closed by a wall with a central fountain set on a long terrace, as in the brief and the subsequent plan proposed by the architects (fig. 149). In 2005, the Howard Foundation offered to fund a tiered auditorium in the form of a theatre, which was accepted by the College on the condition that the Foundation would pay for all direct and indirect costs associated with the project. In 2007 a deed of gift was completed once the Foundation had sold its main commercial asset, its "Cambridge Diet" business in entirety, and both parties had approved detailed plans for the project. This resulted in a re-think of how to accommodate a further major building into this composition on what was now an almost full site.

The Howard Theatre (2008–10) is the most recent addition to the architecture of Downing College (figs. 147 and 150–161), designed by Quinlan and Francis Terry in collaboration with the London-based Theatre Projects Consultants then simultaneously working on the Oslo Opera House. Again built of Ketton stone, this building continued the original feature of the court with the Doric colonnade running along its north side facing the Howard Building across the sunken lawn (fig. 147). In order to accommodate such a substantial building into the existing layout of Howard Court, the new Theatre

148

148. The stone griffin, East Lodge Garden.
149. Plan of the former West Lodge Garden Quadrangle, now Howard Court. Plan Courtesy of Quinlan & Francis Terry Architects

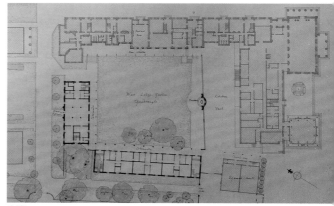

149

150. *Ceiling, Howard Theatre.*

152

151 (previous pages). Howard Theatre auditorium at stalls level.

152 and 153. Auditorium at the upper level showing balcony seating.

153

154

154. Luxury seating in the Howard Theatre.

155. Painting of Parnassus after Anton Mengs on the coved ceiling of the Howard Theatre, by Ian Cairnie.

156. Trompe l'oeil griffin composition on the coved ceiling of the Howard Theatre, by Francis Terry.

155

156

157

157–159. Howard Theatre safety curtain as the Downing Acropolis, painted by Francis Terry, 2009. Preparatory sketch and explanatory diagram. Sketch and diagram courtesy of Quinlan & Francis Terry Architects.

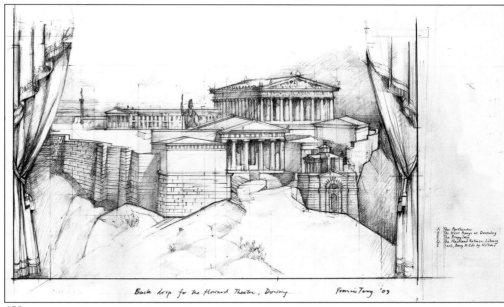

158

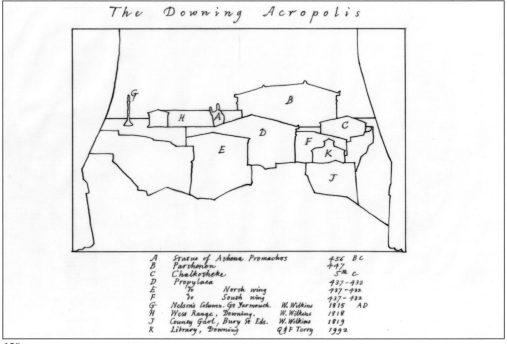

159

160 and 161. The Grace Howard reception room, Howard Theatre.

had to sit partly within the kitchen service yard and also protrude into the court space, unfortunately compromising Howard Lodge by awkwardly overlapping its south end and interrupting the east–west symmetry of the whole composition (e.g. fig. 147). This must have been a most frustrating compromise for the architects to impose on the court; but what was sacrificed externally, is more than made up for in the extraordinary interior which has given the College one of the most exquisite small modern theatres in Britain (figs. 150-7, pp. 137-44).

The Howard Theatre was modelled on the Georgian Theatre Royal of Richmond, Yorkshire, of 1788, and that of Bury St Edmunds, Suffolk, of 1819. The latter was designed by William Wilkins, just after his work at Downing. The interior, by Francis Terry, is an admirable achievement, based mainly on the restored theatre in Bury, one of the last surviving Georgian playhouses still in use. It employs complex geometry to create an ideal theatrical space, based on proportional theory that, as Terry states: "has always excited architects, from ancient Egypt to Le Corbusier and his Modular man. It is sometimes seen as the philosopher's stone of architecture, the secret ingredient that turns dull construction into a work of sublime beauty. In the classical tradition a commonly held belief is that simple number ratios (eg 1:1, 4:3, 3:2) give an inherently pleasing effect. This idea goes back to Plato's *Timaeus* which suggests the pattern of numbers that structures the harmony of the universe can be seen in other types of harmony. From this, the proportions of man, architecture and music were thought to share the same numerical compositions."[11] The interior also contains some outstanding paintings by Francis Terry and the leading *trompe l'œil* artist, Ian Cairnie, in the coves of the ceiling, on the ceiling itself, and the delightful "Downing Acropolis" painting on the safety curtain (figs. 157-59, pp. 144-5). The red leather seating (fig. 154) was chosen by a small group from the College, including Dr Howard, on a visit to the factory of the Italian furniture designers Poltrona Frau, a company which also produces high-end leather interiors for expensive Italian sports cars. Apparently, Dr Howard sat in a sample seat for more than an hour to ensure comfort over long periods. These luxurious seats provide 120 of the 160 seating capacity. The Theatre is also a great "green" example of Downing's commitment to energy conservation and carbon reduction, having a ground-source heat pump system installed in the sunken garden next to it, providing the Theatre's heating and cooling needs all year round; a 10,000-litre rainwater collection storage tank under a herb garden nearby that satisfies its water requirements; and solar water-heating panels on the roof heating all hot water in the building. The creatively planted sunken garden of Howard Court (figs. 145 and 147) was made possible by a generous donation from the alumnus Sir Gordon Rees through the Malabar Trust.

162 and 163. Richmond House to Regent Street and backing onto the College.

164. The Lord Butterfield Building, as the Junior Combination Room.

162

163

164

The three other Terry buildings at Downing, built between 1987 and 1992, are all located in the opposite north-eastern corner of the site near the entrance: Richmond House (1987–9), a commercial office block facing onto Regent Street (figs. 162 and 163); the Butterfield Building as the Junior Combination Room bar/café/party room (1987–9, figs. 164 and 165); and the long-awaited College Library of 1990–3.

When the new Maitland Robinson Library was opened in November 1993 by H.R.H. the Prince of Wales and H.R.H. the Duchess of Kent, Patron of the College, the celebrations marked, at last, the first purpose-built Library in the College's 193-year history (figs. 166-177). Wilkins' original Library would have shared the magnificent South Range with the Chapel, occupying the western half towards the Hall (see fig. 75, p. 66); and Baker's intended Library in the early 1930s would have similarly flanked the Chapel to its east in the centre of the new North Range (see fig. 109, pp. 98-9); both prime locations, but neither built. After almost two centuries of building activity, there was not much space remaining in the immediate area of the domus. The location ultimately chosen, just forward of the main entrance gates and Porters' Lodge from Regent Street, was the perfect siting for the Library, and it has given the entrance to the College a new focal strength on approach to the main quadrangle. With its dominant Greek overtones, especially the main Doric portico to the south, the Library in this location echoes Wilkins' original, unexecuted entrance composition with Porters' Lodge (see fig. 67, p. 63). In fact, for Quinlan Terry at this time in the early 1990s – a decidedly Roman classical architect – we see a definite swing towards the Greek, so perhaps his first decade working around Wilkins at Downing was beginning to rub off.

The composition and main elevation of the Library are very much along the lines of a Palladian villa, with a simple square plan but punctuated by strong Greek elements: the main Tetrastyle portico to the south; a secondary projection to the east, largely concealed by a large fir tree; and the octagonal stairwell rising through the centre of the building. All three components have clearly identifiable Athenian sources: the south portico is derived from the gateway into the Roman Agora; the eastern side projection is based on the now largely destroyed Choragic Monument of Thrasyllus on the Acropolis; and the octagonal stairwell projecting through the roof and topped with a finial capital is after the Tower of the Winds.[12] A pleasing decorative feature are the carvings in the metopes (the square spaces) around the frieze of the south portico, depicting subjects studied at Downing, ranging from the traditional symbols for Law and Medicine, through to the more modern double-helix representing Biology (figs. 168-9).

165. *The Lord Butterfield Cafe and Bar.*

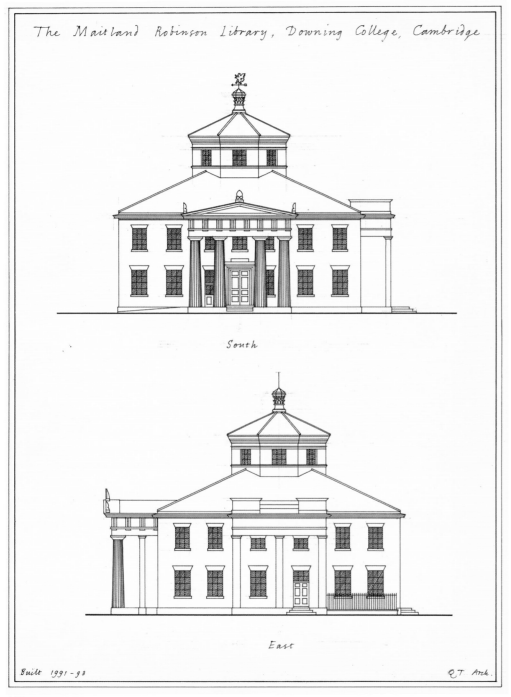

The Maitland Robinson Library, Downing College, Cambridge

South

East

Built 1991-93

QT. Arch.

166

166 and 167. The Maitland Robinson Library, with drawing of elevations by the architects. Drawing courtesy of Quinlan & Francis Terry Architects.

167

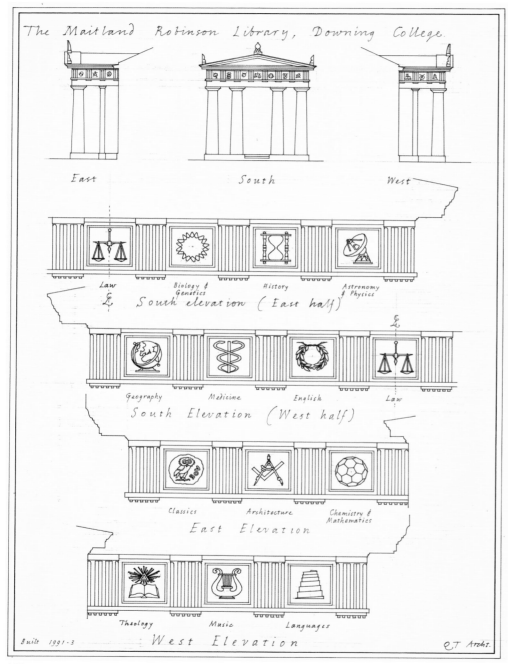

168 and 169. Examination subjects studied at Downing depicted in the portico frieze of the Maitland Robinson Library, with a drawing by the architects. Drawing courtesy of Quinlan & Francis Terry Architects.

168

169

172. 170–2 The Maitland Robinson Library staircase.

Tower of the Winds
Choragic Monument of Thrasyllas } Athens
Portico of Augustus

Maitland Robinson Library

D   Medici Chapel, Florence   Francis Terry
E   Osterton House, Notts
F   Fitzwilliam Museum, Cambridge

173

174

173. Depiction by the architect, Francis Terry, of the Maitland Robinson Library in the style of Piranesi, showing Classical influences for the design. Courtesy of Quinlan & Francis Terry Architects.

174 and 175. Plasterwork designed by Francis Terry for the staircase of the Maitland Robinson Library, shown in a working drawing by the architect using the griffin from the Downing coat of arms. Courtesy of Quinlan & Francis Terry Architects.

175

The Library is of load-bearing Ketton stone, two storeys arranged around the central staircase with a basement. Quinlan Terry worked here with another architect, Harry Faulkner-Brown (1920–2008), the international library specialist, who was responsible for the technical specification and suggested the simple square plan of bookcases in the centre with readers located around the perimeter, for a capacity of 30,000 to 40,000 volumes. The main internal feature is the staircase (figs. 170-2), in the upper part of which are a number of beautifully executed stucco reliefs by Francis Terry using the Downing griffin and other heraldic beasts (figs. 174 and 175), and the surrounding study areas and bookstacks are under shallow coffered ceilings (fig. 177).

An interesting feature of all the Ketton-stone Terry buildings in Downing is that the architect specified that there were to be no pink or blue/grey Ketton blocks, as seen on many of the older buildings elsewhere in the College.[13] This gives the Howard Court buildings and the Library, in particular, a very refined and purist appearance when compared to their more multi-hued neighbours.

Notes
1 Bicknell, *Aspects*, pp. 15–16.
2 He is not to be confused with the other Cambridge TV rental millionaire, David Robinson, founder of Robinson College.
3 Sicca, p. 104.
4 Ibid.
5 Ibid., p. 105.
6 Watkin, *Radical Classicism*, p. 9.
7 Interview with Quinlan and Francis Terry, Dedham, Essex, 20 May 2015.
8 Ibid.
9 Sicca, p. 105.
10 Watkin, *Radical Classicism*, p. 226.
11 Francis Terry, "Magic Numbers", *RIBA Journal*, November 2007, p. 42.
12 Watkin, *Radical Classicism*, p. 230.
13 Conversation with Quinlan Terry, 29 July 2015.

176

177. Bookstacks, Maitland Robinson Library.   176. (facing page) Weather-vane, Maitland Robinson Library.

178

6 Recent projects

Restoration of the Hall – Caruso St John Architects 2005–9

In the academic year 1998–9 the Kettle's Yard artist-in-residence, Stephen Chambers, was accommodated at Downing and had a studio just down the road at Christ's College. While Stephen was accessible to all in the University, he became a particularly familiar face in the College and has contributed much to its artistic activity and development ever since. So valuable has been his involvement that he was made an Honorary Fellow in 2015.

An idea from the time of his residency to "repaint the Hall" arose[1] and, in the early years of the new millennium, this idea developed into a more committed approach for a thorough restoration project of this Grade I listed building. This included an upgrade of the back-of-house facilities in that area – the kitchens, offices and Fellows' amenities – something which had not been addressed since the new, modernist buildings were constructed in the late 1960s by Howell, Killick, Partridge & Amis. The main aim of the project was to restore the Hall interior as accurately as possible to how Wilkins might have intended it. Introduced to the College by Chambers, the firm of Caruso St John Architects, working with a number of specialist consultants, achieved the impressive transformation of the Hall and vastly improved the surrounding facilities on both ground and upper floors, including adjustment and re-planning of the internal spaces and some new extensions. The first phase of the works dealing with all the service spaces surrounding the Hall was completed in 2007, encompassing the replacement of the old kitchens, a new servery and bar, and new administrative offices. The second phase, focusing on the Hall itself, began in 2008, and not only upgraded all the services associated with the essential functions of this core component of the College's daily life, but also embarked on the painstakingly complex process of discovering what lay beneath the accretions of two hundred years of the building's history. This began by the endless scraping and stripping back of layers of previous refurbishments, the last of these undertaken in the 1960s by HKPA and the specialist interiors firm Colefax and Fowler. These new site investigations, along with historical research, revealed the original Georgian palette of the polychrome interior and the remarkable Greek Revival ornament of the early nineteenth century. Frustrating gaps in the historical record required informed and creative invention from the architects,

178. Ionic heads and entablature detail in the Hall.

and root sources for similar interiors of the same period were referenced and visited, such as Robert Adam's Syon House, Isleworth, Middlesex (1762–9); the Sir John Soane Museum, London (1792–1824); and even 1820s and 1830s interiors of the great German Greek Revivalist architect, Karl Friedrich Schinkel. The resulting interior is a superb example of what the original architect had probably wished for, based on archaeological fact and sound historical research. The furniture and chandeliers, all designed by the architects, were derived from Greek sources. A total of 756 donors contributed to this most recent restoration of the Hall.

Note
1 Interview with Stephen Chambers, 15 July 2015.

179. Composition showing the previous colour scheme in the Hall. Image created by Caruso St John Architects from photographs by Ioana Marinescu.

180-185. The results of the restoration:

180. Entablature detail, east end of the Hall.

181. The north wall.

182. Entablature detail of the north wall.

183. View looking east.

184. Wide view to south-east.

185. Wide view to west.

179

180

181

182

186-8. The College Boathouse by David Thurlow Architects. Opened in 2001, it also provides some graduate accommodation on the upper floor.

186

187

188

189

189-90. Singer Building, by Bland, Brown & Cole Architects. Opened in 2000, providing graduate accommodation in this leafy corner of the College site.

190

191

191-3. Griphon House. Conversion of existing building into student accommodation by Robert Lombardelli Partnership, opened in 2012.

194

194–6. *Restoration of the West Lodge and Music Room in the West Range, by Henry Freeland, architect, working with Sir Peter Thornton. In honour of Tim Cadbury's many contributions to the College.*

195

196

197. The Heong Gallery (exhibition: "The Court of Redonda", by Stephen Chambers RA)

198. First Court and Battcock Lodge.

199. The Heong Gallery as the west side of First Court.

The Parker's House project, completed in 2016, involved the conversion of the former commercial building fronting onto Regent Street into student and conference accommodation, along with the creation of the new First Court and a public art gallery. The main building was renamed Battcock Lodge (fig. 198), in ackowledgement of the generous benefaction of Humphrey Battcock (alumnus 1973). First Court (fig. 198) was made possible by the benefaction of Mr Gifford Combs, a graduate of Harvard and Cambridge universities. The Heong Gallery (figs 197 and 199) is named after Alwyn Heong (alumnus 1979), benefactor. All buildings were by Caruso St John Architects and Robert Lombardelli Partnership.

200. Graduation.

Looking ahead

The archives of Oxford and Cambridge colleges are replete with the unfulfilled dreams and visions of many architects. "In universities, as elsewhere, architecture is always a compromise between the visionary and the practicable," wrote Howard Colvin in 1983, when referring to historical Oxford as "a graveyard of rejected designs".[1] Neither Wilkins nor Baker at Downing produced rejected designs, of course; on the contrary they were magnificent ideas of their time received with much excitement and enthusiasm, but only to be defeated by the frustrations of insufficient funding, the bane of many great artists.

When one looks at Downing's chequered architectural history and thwarted early plans, one can only sympathise with William Wilkins, the originator of the radical and brilliant concept for his new College, and then do the same again when Sir Herbert Baker in the late 1920s tried to give the College something equally dramatic on the by-then-compromised site. Through no fault of their own, both architects failed to realise their visions for Downing, and we have seen through their drawings and models in this book how even more astounding the College might have been if only finances had allowed (see chapters 3 and 4).

In the last half-century the additions to Downing's architecture have been exciting and healthy in respect of its long classical tradition, though inevitably controversial, for on such matters it is impossible to please all camps. Generous benefactions from many alumni devoted to their alma mater – particularly the exceptional gifts of Dr Alan Howard of the Howard Foundation, and Mr Joseph Maitland Robinson – along with the ever more successful financial management of the College over recent years with its special focus on new sources of revenue such as conferences and other functions, have enabled a continuum of building activity that has spurred the College forward more than in any other period since its foundation on 22 September 1800.

There has been a remarkable sequence of projects since the late 1960s (see the timeline, pp. 186–193), as if momentum has been slowly building, and peaks have been achieved: Bill Howell's Senior Combination Room (1965–9); the many buildings of Quinlan and Francis Terry, including the Howard Building, the Howard Theatre and the Maitland Robinson Library (1985–2011); the magnificent restoration of the Hall by Caruso St John Architects (2008–9); and more recently Battcock Lodge, First Court and the Heong Art Gallery (2014–16). For the first time all students can be accommodated on the domus, a major step forward but one still faithful to Wilkins' vision of a spacious and elegant college in which to live and study that remains as relevant today as it did two centuries ago. But what about the Downing that should have been: could something truly magnificent still be waiting to be achieved; something to help lay Wilkins' ghost to rest?

The drawing overleaf shows the beautiful site of today, but with Wilkins' unexecuted South Range in place (fig. 201). This exciting concept would pose many questions, of course, not least what the style of "classical" would be if such a building were ever possible: a modernist reinvention, perhaps, along the lines of Bill Howell's SCR; or a classicist reinterpretation, as with the Terry buildings? Could this fascinating classical adventure ever be concluded in such a grand manner, or sadly remain no more than a flight of fancy. . . .

Note
1 Colvin, p. vii.

201. The College of the future?
Drawing by Ed Rawle © and Blackpoint Design

TIMELINE

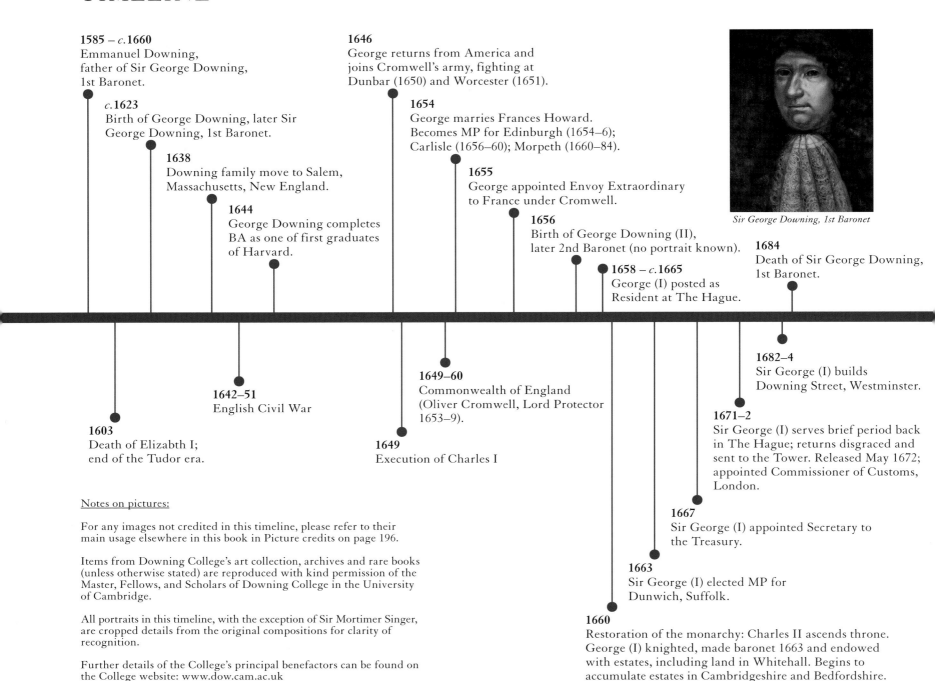

1585 – c.1660
Emmanuel Downing,
father of Sir George Downing,
1st Baronet.

c.1623
Birth of George Downing, later Sir
George Downing, 1st Baronet.

1638
Downing family move to Salem,
Massachusetts, New England.

1644
George Downing completes
BA as one of first graduates
of Harvard.

1646
George returns from America and
joins Cromwell's army, fighting at
Dunbar (1650) and Worcester (1651).

1654
George marries Frances Howard.
Becomes MP for Edinburgh (1654–6);
Carlisle (1656–60); Morpeth (1660–84).

1655
George appointed Envoy Extraordinary
to France under Cromwell.

1656
Birth of George Downing (II),
later 2nd Baronet (no portrait known).

1658 – c.1665
George (I) posted as
Resident at The Hague.

1684
Death of Sir George Downing,
1st Baronet.

Sir George Downing, 1st Baronet

1682–4
Sir George (I) builds
Downing Street, Westminster.

1671–2
Sir George (I) serves brief period back
in The Hague; returns disgraced and
sent to the Tower. Released May 1672;
appointed Commissioner of Customs,
London.

1667
Sir George (I) appointed Secretary to
the Treasury.

1663
Sir George (I) elected MP for
Dunwich, Suffolk.

1660
Restoration of the monarchy: Charles II ascends throne.
George (I) knighted, made baronet 1663 and endowed
with estates, including land in Whitehall. Begins to
accumulate estates in Cambridgeshire and Bedfordshire.

1642–51
English Civil War

1603
Death of Elizabth I;
end of the Tudor era.

1649–60
Commonwealth of England
(Oliver Cromwell, Lord Protector
1653–9).

1649
Execution of Charles I

Sir George Downing, 3rd Baronet and Founder of Downing College

Mary Forester, Lady Mary Downing, wife of the 3rd Baronet

Sir Jacob Garrard Downing, 4th and last Baronet

Margaret Bowyer, Lady Margaret Downing, wife of the 4th Baronet

Francis Annesley, the first Master of Downing College

1685
Birth of George Downing (III).

1700 Marriage of George Downing III (15) to his cousin, Mary Forrester (13).

1764
Bill lodged in Court of Chancery on behalf of Cambridge University, petitioning for the creation of the College. Lady Downing continues to argue entitlement; costly litigation ensues.

1764
Death of Sir Jacob Garrard Downing, 4th Baronet, childless and last living male heir. Sir Jacob's will named his wife as executrix, who assumes inheritance of the estates, disregarding the will of 1717.

*c.***1778–9**
Francis Annesley MP, great-grandson of Sir George Downing I, champions the Downing cause and becomes first Master.

1749: 10 June
Death of Sir George Downing, 3rd Baronet, succeeded by his cousin, Sir Jacob Garrard Downing.

1778
Birth of William Wilkins, eventual architect of Downing.

1734
Death of Lady Mary Downing (Mary Forester).

1778
Death of Lady Margaret Downing. Litigation continues against her heirs, greatly eroding value of the estates.

1717: 20 December
Will of Sir George Downing III stating that if his four named heirs should die without issue his estate to be used to found "Downings Colledge" in the University of Cambridge.

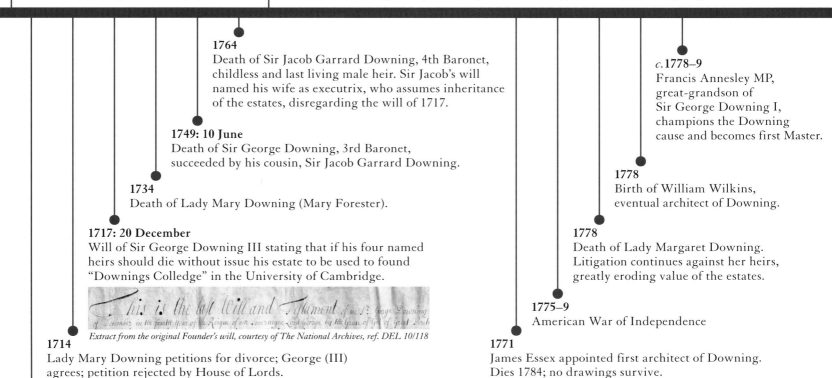

Extract from the original Founder's will, courtesy of The National Archives, ref. DEL 10/118

1775–9
American War of Independence

1714
Lady Mary Downing petitions for divorce; George (III) agrees; petition rejected by House of Lords.

1771
James Essex appointed first architect of Downing. Dies 1784; no drawings survive.

1711
Death of Sir George Downing, 2nd Baronet.

187

1784
King George III, "the architect King", requests the design of the new college to be in the classical style, not Gothic. James Wyatt appointed architect by Francis Annesley.

1800: 22 September
Royal Charter granted to Downing College. First governing body and small fellowship established under Annesley as Master.

1801–7
Purchase of the College site Pembroke Leys.

1803–15
Napoleonic Wars

1801–04
Wilkins does his 'grand tour' visiting Greece, Asia Minor (modern-day Turkey) and Italy; fascinated by archaeological investigation. On return sets up in practice as an architect.

Downing Folio I

The Temple of Concord, one of many plates from Wilkins' The Antiquities of Magna Graecia *published in 1807*

1796
Wilkins enters Gonville & Caius College to read mathematics, graduating in 1800.

1789–99
French Rovolution

1804
First scheme for the new College proposed by James Wyatt. The Master of the Court of Chancery halts proceedings, requesting a second scheme be sought.

The first proposal for the design of Downing College by James Wyatt (1746–1813)

1805: February
George Byfield submits designs for the College, unseats Wyatt as the architect of Downing.

The second proposal for Downing by George Byfield (c.1756–1813)

1805: April
Byfield and Wilkins exhibit their drawings at the Royal Academy. Within the year further proposals by Francis Sandys (none survive) and William Porden.

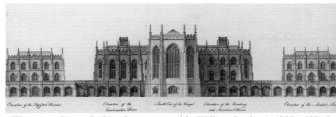

The extraordinary Gothic scheme proposed by William Porden (c.1755–1822) for the design of Downing, in defiance of the King's wishes

1805: 23 July
First College statutes, rules and ordinances published.

1805: 21 October
Battle of Trafalgar

1805: December
Fellowship reject schemes of Byfield, Sandys and Porden. Lewis William Wyatt puts forward a proposal. Wilkins and Wyatt asked to adjust and resubmit.

The final submission for the design of Downing by Lewis William Wyatt (1777–1853)

1806: March
Panel of eminent architect judges established to select between the schemes of Wilkins and Wyatt. Wilkins wins the commission, the first example in collegiate architecture of the spacious campus plan.

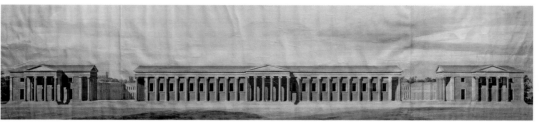

The winning proposal for Downing by William Wilkins, showing the south range buildings of Hall, Library and Chapel, and Master's Lodge

William Wilkins, Architect of Downing (1778–1839)

1806–7
Building begins on east range; foundation stone laid 18 May 1807.

1811
Master's Lodge and East Lodge completed.

The Master's Lodge, the first completed building of the College, with the centre of Cambridge beyond

1837
Wilkins elected Royal Academy Professor of Architecture.

1839
Death of William Wilkins, Architect of Downing College.

1825
The West Field allocated as the Fellows' Garden.

1821
A room above west end of Hall designated for use as a chapel.

1837
Victoria ascends throne.

1812
Death of Francis Annesley: succeeded by William Frere as 2nd Master of Downing

1818–21
West Range built, including the Hall and the West Lodge.

1836
Death of William Frere: succeeded by Thomas Worsley as 3rd Master of Downing.

William Frere, Master of Downing 1812–36

The West Range, showing the Hall, Chambers and West Lodge as the house for the Downing Professor of the Laws of England

1817
Admission of first undergraduate.

1813
Completion of chambers between the Master's Lodge and East Lodge.

Thomas Worsley, Master of Downing 1836–85

1834
Small house built towards Regent Street, later to become the Porters' Lodge.

The East Range, showing the chambers between the East Lodge, as the house for the Downing Professor of Medicine, and the Master's Lodge

The Porters' Lodge today

189

North end of the East Range

North end of the West Range

1873–6
Completion of the East and West Ranges by Edward Middleton Barry, Architect

1893
Tchaikovsky stays in West Lodge for a concert to mark the 50th anniversary of the Cambridge University Musical Society.

Photograph 1891 Boat Club Trials (DCPH/8/1)

Revd. J. C. Saunders

1895
Two acres of the site adjoining Downing Street sold to the University.

Development of the Lensfield Road boundary with the building of large red-brick houses let on 99-year leases.

The Lensfield Road villas forming the southern boundary to the College site

Portrait by Herbert James Gunn, 1933

Sir Albert Charles Seward, Master of Downing 1915–36

1915
Death of Howard Marsh: succeeded by Sir Albert Charles Seward as 7th Master of Downing.

1885
Death of Thomas Worsley: succeeded by Professor William Lloyd Birkbeck as 4th Master of Downing.

1888
Death of William Birkbeck: succeeded by Professor Alexander Hill as 5th Master of Downing.

1893–5
Revd. J. C. Saunders, Tutor and Chaplain, privately purchases plot of land on Lower River including Waite's boathouse. New front added to existing building, creating Downing's first boathouse (dem. 1999). Saunders conveys site to the College in December 1895.

1907
Death of Alex Hill: succeeded by Professor Frederick Howard Marsh as 6th Master of Downing.

1924
Death of Sidney Wynn Graystone, leaving the eventual residue of his estate to Downing on the death of his widow in 1945. Provides impetus to pursue much needed buildings.

Portrait by Miss Bond, n.d.

William Lloyd Birkbeck, Master of Downing 1885–8

Portrait by Miss Emily Humphrey, c.1891

Alex Hill, Master of Downing 1888–1907

Ref: DCPP/FLE/5/2

The original College Boathouse, c.1895

1897–1901
Sale of remaining land in the northern area of the site to the University, leading to creation of the modern Downing Site laboratory precinct.

Portrait by Alfred Page, c.1953

Frederick Howard Marsh, Master of Downing 1907–15

Photographic portrait, picture no. 075

Sidney Wynn Graystone (alumnus 1882)

1929
The College engages the eminent colonial architect Sir Herbert Baker to advise on the development of the northern area of the site.

1931–2
Completion of Baker's east and west corner wings of the North Range.

Sir Herbert Baker's North Range from the south-east

1950–3
North Range completed by the Graystone Buildings, the central section including the Chapel.

The Chapel

Kenny Court

Portrait by Edward Clegg Wilkinson, c.1909

Courtney Stanhope Kenny (1847–1930)

1960–3
Kenny Court, named after Professor Kenny, via a bequest from his daughters Agnes and Gertrude.

Portrait by John Ward, c.1976

Sir Morien Bedford Morgan, Master of Downing 1972–8

1972
Retirement of William Guthrie: succeeded by Sir Morien Bedford Morgan as 11th Master of Downing.

Portrait by Margaret Virginia Foreman, 1983

Sir John Butterfield, Master of Downing 1978–87

1978
Death of Morien Morgan: succeeded by Professor Sir William John Hughes Butterfield as 12th Master of Downing.

1936
Retirement of Albert Seward: succeeded by Admiral Sir Herbert William Richmond as 8th Master of Downing

Portrait by Henry Lamb, 1944

Sir Herbert Richmond, Master of Downing 1936–46

1946
Death of Herbert Richmond: succeeded by Professor Sir Lionel Ernest Howard Whitby as 9th Master of Downing

Portrait by Waldron West, 1957

Sir Lionel Whitby, Master of Downing 1946–57

1956
Death of Lionel Whitby: succeeded by Professor William Keith Chambers Guthrie as 10th Master of Downing

Portrait by Kenneth Green, c.1967

Professor William Guthrie, Master of Downing 1957–72

1966
Legacy of Sir Adam Mortimer Singer, via the death of his widow, provides further impetus for major building projects.

© National Portrait Gallery, London

Sir Adam Mortimer Singer (alumnus 1881)

1966–72
New Senior Combination Room, Kitchens and Offices by Howell, Killick, Partridge & Amis.

The Senior Combination Room (SCR)

Interior of the SCR

1984
Completion of Parker's House commercial development to Regent Street by Nicholas Ray Architects (now Battcock Lodge).

1978
First female Fellow admitted to Downing.

1980
First female students admitted to Downing.

Dr Alan Howard (alumnus 1948) and Jon Howard (1974), founding trustees of The Howard Foundation

Portrait by Peter Edwards, 1990

Peter Mathias, Master of Downing 1987–95

1987
Retirement of John Butterfield: succeeded by Professor Peter Mathias as 13th Master of Downing.

Howard Lodge

1992–4
Howard Court built by the addition of a west range south of the Howard Building. Later renamed Howard Lodge with the creation and naming of the 'Court'. By Quinlan & Francis Terry.

David Anthony King, Master of Downing 1995–2000

1995
Retirement of Peter Mathias: succeeded by Professor David Anthony King as 14th Master of Downing.

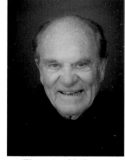

Portrait by Dick Smyly, c.2001 (courtesy of the artist)

Stephen George Fleet, Master of Downing 2001–3

2000
Resignation of David King: succeeded by Dr Stephen George Fleet as 15th Master of Downing.

1984
Deed of Gift from the Howard Foundation for construction of the Howard Building, the first of three Howard Foundation buildings eventually forming Howard Court.

1985–7
Howard Building, by Quinlan Terry.

Howard Building, north elevation

1991–3
Maitland Robinson Library, after Mr Joseph Maitland Robinson, benefactor. By Quinlan & Francis Terry with Harry Faulkner-Brown.

The Maitland Robinson Library

Flemming Heilmann (alumnus 1979)

1987–8
Richmond House commercial development to Regent Street, and Butterfield Building as new Junior Common Room and Café. Both by Quinlan Terry.

Portrait by Richard Stone, 1991 (courtesy of the artist)

Joseph Maitland Robinson (alumnus 1925)

1999–2000
Singer Building, by Bland, Brown & Cole. Named after Sir Mortimer Singer, whose legacy in the 1960s had been so important for the College. Also enabled by the generous support of Flemming Heilmann.

Butterfield Building

Singer Building

The new Boathouse

2000–01
New Downing Boathouse by
David Thurlow Architects.
Funded by the generous support
of members of the 1971 Men's
1st VIII and more than 240
other Downing men and women,
with the help of Chris Bartram.

*Chris Bartram
(alumnus 1968)*

Griphon House

2011–12
Conversion of
Griphon House into
student and conference
accommodation by
Robert Lombardelli
Partnership.

2014–16
Conversion of Parker's
House commercial
property to Battcock
Lodge residential
building by Caruso St
John Architects and
Robert Lombardelli
Partnership. Named
after Humphrey
Battcock, benefactor,
with the help of Chris
Bartram and others.

*Humphrey Battcock
(alumnus 1973)*

*Alan Bookbinder,
Master of Downing 2018–*

2018
Retirement of
Geoffrey Grimmett:
succeeded by Mr Alan
Bookbinder as 18th
Master of Downing.

Battcock Lodge and First Court

2003
Retirement of Stephen
Fleet: succeeded by
Professor Barry John
Everitt as 16th Master
of Downing.

2008–10
Howard Theatre built as south
range of Howard Court.
By Quinlan & Francis Terry.

2013
Retirement of Barry
Everitt: succeeded by
Professor Geoffrey
Richard Grimmett as
17th Master of Downing.

2014–16
First Court at north
end of Battcock
Lodge by benefaction
of Gifford Combs.

2014–16
Heong Gallery, named after
Mr Alwyn Heong (alumnus
1979), benefactor. By Caruso
St John Architects.

Portrait by Paul Brason, 2007 (courtesy of the artist)

*Barry John Everitt, Master
of Downing 2003–13*

The Howard Theatre

2007–9
Restoration of the Hall
by Caruso St John
Architects. Made possible
by major gifts from
Tim Cadbury (alumnus
1951) and Richard
Williams, with the help
of Chris Bartram and
supported by donations
from 750 others.

Photograph by Bruce Head ©

*Geoffrey Richard Grimmett,
Master of Downing 2013–18*

Gifford Combs

Alwyn Heong

*Richard Williams
(alumnus 1967)*

Heong Gallery

Restoration of the Hall

193

202. The College site and its surroundings, May 2014.

Bibliography

Bicknell, Peter, "The Development of the College Buildings", in *Aspects of Downing History* (Stanley French [ed.]), Cambridge, Downing College Association, 1982, pp. 2–18.

Bolitho, Hector, *No. 10 Downing Street, 1660–1900*, London, Hutchinson, 1957.

Bradley, Simon, and Nikolaus Pevsner, *The Buildings of England: Cambridgeshire* New Haven and London, Yale University Press, 2014.

Colvin, Howard, *A Biographical Dictionary of British Architects 1600–1840* London, John Murray, 1978.

Colvin, Howard, *Unbuilt Oxford*, New Haven and London, Yale University Press, 1983.

Evelyn, John (E. S. de Beer, ed.), *The Diary of John Evelyn*, volume III *Kalendarium* Oxford, Oxford University Press, 2000.

Fitzwilliam Museum, *The Age of Wilkins: The Architecture of Improvement*, Cambridge, Fitzwilliam Museum, 2000.

French, Stanley, *The History of Downing College, Cambridge* Cambridge, Downing College Association, 1978.

Henderson, W. Otto, "The College Estates", in *Aspects of Downing History* (Stanley French [ed.]), Cambridge, Downing College Association, 1982.

Hope, Thomas, *Observations on the Plans and Elevations Designed by James Wyatt, Architect, for Downing College, Cambridge; in a Letter to Francis Annesley, Esq., M.P.*, printed by D. N. Shury, London, 1804.

Liscombe, R. W. (1980). *William Wilkins, 1778–1839*. Cambridge, Cambridge University Press, 1980.

Peirce, Benjamin, *A History of Harvard University, from Its Foundation, in the Year 1636, to the Period of the American Revolution* Cambridge, Mass., 1833.

Pepys, Samuel, *The Diaries of Samuel Pepys* (1633–1703).

Pettit Stevens, H. W., *Downing College* London, F. E. Robinson. 1899.

Pevsner, Nikolaus, *The Buildings of England: Cambridgeshire*, 2nd edn. New Haven & London, Yale University Press, 2002.

Saumarez Smith, Otto, "A Strange, Brutalist 'Primitive Hut': Howell, Killick, Partridge and Amis's Senior Combination Room at Downing College, Cambridge", in *Oxford and Cambridge* (Elain Harwood, Alan Powers and Otto Saumarez Smith, eds.), *Twentieth-Century Architecture 11* London, Twentieth Century Society, 2013, pp. 148–65 2014.

Shallard, Patrick, "Sir George Downing, first baronet, 1623–1684", in *Aspects of Downing History* (Stanley French [ed.]) Cambridge, Downing College Association, 1982, pp. 119–33.

Sicca, Cinzia Maria, with contributions by Charles Harpum and Edward Powell; photography by Tim Rawle, *Committed to Classicism: The Building of Downing College, Cambridge* Cambridge, Downing College, 1987.

Simmons, Frederick Johnson, *Narrative Outline for a Biography of Emanuel Downinge, 1585-1660* Portland, Maine, Forest City Printing Company, 1958.

Summerson, John, *The Classical Language of Architecture* London, Thames & Hudson, 1980.

Watkin, David, *The Architect King: George III and the Culture of the Enlightenment* London, Royal Collection Publications, 2004

Watkin, David, *The Practice of Classical Architecture: The Architecture of Quinlan and Francis Terry, 2005–2015* Rizzoli, New York, 2015.

Watkin, David, *Radical Classicism: The Architecture of Quinlan Terry* New York, Rizzoli, 2006.

Willis, Robert, and John Willis Clark, *The Architectural History of the University of Cambridge, and of the Colleges of Cambridge and Eton*, 1886 (4 vols.).

Picture credits

Jeremy Bays, figs. 5, 64–5, 200

Caruso St John Architects, figs. 179 (and Ioana Marinescu), 197–8

Items from Downing College art collection and archives are reproduced with kind permission of the **Master, Fellows, and Scholars of Downing College** in the University of Cambridge.

Art Collection:

Fig. 38: Lady (Mary) Downing (1687–1734), wife of Sir George Downing, 3rd Bt, by Michael Dahl, c. 1705

Fig. 39: Sir George Downing (1685–1749), 3rd Bt, Founder, by John Theodore Heins, 1751

Fig. 42: Lady (Margaret) Downing, wife of Sir Jacob Downing, 4th Bt, by Thomas Gainsborough

Fig. 43: Francis Annesley (1734–1812) by Christopher Adams (after Karl Anton Hickel)

Fig. 61: Marble bust of William Wilkins after bust by Edward Hodges Baily

Figs. 68–75: Model of Wilkins' concept for Downing College (Andrew Ingham Associates, London), made for "The Age of Wilkins" (Fitzwilliam Museum exhibition, 2000)

Fig. 85: Aquatint of the Hall, Downing College, n.d.

Fig. 107: Perspective of proposed new building, Downing College, by C. G. Hare, 1914

Archive:

Fig. 30: *Collegium Dunense* etching of the Master's Lodge, n.d. (DCAR/1/2/2/1/1/183)

Fig. 44: "Downing College, as it will appear when completed", etching by J. Le Keux after F. Mackenzie, 1842 (DCAR/1/2/2/1/1/184)

Fig. 45: "A plan of St Thomas's Leys otherwise Pembroke Leys in the Town of Cambridge made on the extinguishing the rights of Common over the same", 1803 (DCAR/1/2/1/D4/3)

Fig. 49: Plan of the site and general plan of the College by George Byfield, 1804 (DCAR/1/2/2/1/3/1)

Fig. 50: Elevation of the Master's Lodge and termination of the west wing by George Byfield, 1804 (DCAR/1/2/2/1/3/8)

Fig. 51: Elevation of the south front with sections of the east and west wings by George Byfield, 1804 (DCAR/1/2/2/1/3/7)

Fig. 57: Plan of Downing site with block plan of College by Lewis William Wyatt, 1805 (DCAR/1/2/2/1/2/1)

Figs. 58–60: Elevation of the east range with sections of triumphal arch and chapel by Lewis William Wyatt, 1805 (DCAR/1/2/2/1/2/6); Elevation of the south front of the north range by Lewis William Wyatt, 1805 (DCAR/1/2/2/1/2/5); Elevation of south front of south range by Lewis William Wyatt, 1805 (DCAR/1/2/2/1/2/7)

Fig. 62: Block plan of Downing College by William Wilkins, n.d. (DCAR/1/2/2/1/1/176)

Fig. 63: South elevation of the South Range by William Wilkins, after 1812 (DCAR/1/2/2/1/1/2)

Fig. 66: Revised plan of the College, 1817-18, showing the entrance composition in the north to Downing Street. (DCAR/1/2/2/1/1/88)

Fig. 76: Section through west end of Chapel by William Wilkins, c.1806. Downing College Archive (DCAR/1/2/2/1/1/3)

Fig. 82: *Downing College*, colour etching by W. Westall and D. Howell, published 1814 for R. Ackermann's *History of Cambridge* (DCHR/1/6/7)

Fig. 83: Plan for the improvement of the estate belonging to Downing College by William Wilkins, 1817 (DCAR/1/2/2/1/1/103)

Fig. 84: Southern half of the general plan of the College by William Wilkins, c.1806 (detail) (DCAR/1/2/2/1/1/89)

Fig. 86: Plan of Downing College and Pleasure Grounds by William Wilkins, 1822 (DCAR/1/2/2/1/1/172)

Fig. 106: The former Chapel room ("Upper Room")

Fig. 108: Aerial perspective from appeal brochure *Downing College: An appeal for funds for the erection of new buildings*, 1930 (DCAR/1/2/5/7)

Fig. 109: Plan and elevation of proposed buildings, from appeal brochure *Downing College: An appeal for funds for the erection of new buildings*, 1930 (DCAR/1/2/5/7)

Fig. 110: Drawing of "The Gateway" from appeal brochure *Downing College: An appeal for funds for the erection of new buildings*, 1930 (DCAR/1/2/5/7)

Fig. 111: Painting of the view of the proposed east-west axis from Regent Street by H. G. Pilkington, 1929, as reproduced in appeal brochure *Downing College: An appeal for funds for the erection of new buildings*, 1930 (DCAR/1/2/5/7)

Fig. 113: Revised ground plan and elevation of the North Range by Sir Herbert Richmond, 1946 (DCAR/1/2/4/1/7)

Fig. 133: Perspective sketch of the proposed kitchen "block" and combination room seen from the Fellows' garden (DCGB/1/5/1)

By kind permission of **Mr P. Fullerton**
Fig. 41: Sir Jacob Downing, 4th Bt, style of Henry Pickering

Harvard Art Museums/Fogg Museum
Fig. 31: Harvard University Portrait Collection, Gift of Harold Murdock to Harvard College, 1925, H347: Portrait of a Man, probably Sir George Downing (1624–1684), after Thomas Smith (d. 1691), by Robert M. Pratt, 1872

Quinlan & Francis Terry Architects, figs. 138, 140, 149, 158–9, 166, 168, 173–5

RIBA Library Drawings and Archives Collections
Figs. 46–8: James Wyatt: Unexecuted designs for Downing College, Cambridge: Perspective from SE [SA44/WYJAS[4]1]; Perspective from NW [SA44/WYJAS[4]2]; Perspective of the courtyard [SA44/WYJAS[4]3]

Figs. 52–3: William Porden: Competition design for Downing College, Cambridge: Rough block plan of the College [SC71/7(2)]; Competition design for Downing College, Cambridge: Plan of the College [SC71/7(16)]

Figs. 54–6: William Porden: Competition design for Downing College, Cambridge: Elevation of the north front [SC71/7(17)]; Elevation of the south front [SC71/7(18)]; Elevation of the east front [SC71/7(19)]

Fig. 67: Colour print by Harraden of Downing College, Cambridge, showing intended entrance to the College from Downing Street [SC182/2(3)]

All other images © **Tim Rawle and Louis Sinclair**, who have donated all their photographs in this book to the Downing College Archive.

Index

203. View of the Paddock to the south-east, with the Master's Lodge to the left and the Catholic Church of Our Lady and the English Martyrs beyond.